BOB DYLAN
On A Couch & Fifty Cents A Day

For
Eve & Mac,
who were there when it Began,
Thanks for Everything,
Love,
Bob

Also, for those who know a little about Bob Dylan, a lot about
Bob Dylan and everyone in between.

BOB DYLAN
On A Couch & Fifty Cents A Day

by

Peter K. McKenzie

MKB
PRESS

BOB DYLAN On A Couch & Fifty Cents A Day
Copyright 2022 by Peter K. McKenzie

First Edition/2021
ISBN 9798503964530

MKB Press
New York
Contact: mkbpnyc@gmail.com

Cover Photograph: Bob Dylan and Howard McKenzie aka "Mac"
Taken by Marcia Stehr
Back Cover Photograph copyright Howard Harrison
Front and Back Cover Design by Katherine Brennan

"I want to be as big as Harry Belafonte." -Bob Dylan 1961

TABLE 0F CONTENTS

INTRODUCTION   11
1. FEBRUARY 16, 1961 - THE FIRST TIME   17
2. THE LUNGS WERE REALY BLOWN OUT   24
3. JACK ELLIOTT   28
4. 1000 MILES FROM HOME   35
5. AFTER GERDE'S   38
6. ALL FIVE   42
7. APRIL 11, 1961 - OPENING NIGHT   50
8. APRIL 21, 1961   57
9. THE COUCH   60
10. TIME FOR BREAKFAST   65
11. 50 CENTS A DAY   72
12. THE RECORDER IS ON   77
13. OUT OF THE BOTTLE   87
14. JUNE 17, 1961 - ABOUT THE CALIFORNIA BROWN
    EYED GIRL   92
15. JUNE 18, 1961   98
16. SHUFFLE THE DECK AND PAPERS   101
17. THE WRESTLER ARRIVES   111
18. 4/12/63 + 18 MONTHS TO RICHARD & MIMI   115
19. A HISTORY LESSON   134
20. ART, ARCHITECTURE, BUT STILL NO THUMBS   144
21. HIJINX IN JULY   152
22. HAROLD LEVENTHAL   160
23. AN ADDITION TO THE SHIP'S CARGO
    MANIFEST   165
24. THE ORIGINAL CARGO MANIFEST   174
25. IT HAPPENED ONE CAMP TIME   181
26. OVER JULY   186
27. TWO IDES IN AUGUST AND ONE IN SEPTEMBER   189
28. BROTHERHOOD OF THE TRAVELING PANTS   193

29. ROLL ON COLUMBIA THROUGH THE
    HURRICANE   200
30. THE AFTERMATH   206
31. TWO YEARS BEFORE THE MAST   212
32. HARD RAIN   219
33. IT'S ALL IN THE FEET   227
34. FIVE DAYS IN '62 AND ONE IN '63   232
35. NOVEMBER 23, 1961 - ANYTHING BUT A
    TURKEY   247
36. GOODBYE IS JUST A SEVEN LETTER WORD   264
    AFTERWORD   270
    FOOTNOTES   272
    ABOUT THE AUTHOR   276
    ACKNOWLEDGEMENTS   277

(My mother and father, Eve and "Mac" McKenzie, at the kitchen table 1950s)

INTRODUCTION

"These are very good people. You can talk to these people. They know me well. You can also talk to Peter. He's old now. Peter goes to Harvard. Peter's their son. It's Eve and Mac McKenzie. And they really took me in an' they were beautiful. Ah, they took me in and I lived with them. And they fed me and it was on 28th St. And I stayed out all hours an' came in and went to sleep on the couch. An' Peter was there. I was his idol. At the time he was about 15. Now he's 18, 19. He's in college. He's a very smart kid. Talk to them."

The above quote is from an interview Bob Dylan did in 1965. I wasn't made aware of it until 30 years later. He made clear with those comments if anyone had any questions, or wanted to fill in the blanks, they should ask us. Despite Bob's advice, we were never contacted by the interviewer...

One afternoon, 60 years ago, my mother asked Bob what he really wanted.
"I want to be as big as Harry Belafonte, Eve," he told her.
That was his desire then. We all know how that wish turned out...

For the spring, summer and beginning of fall 1961 our New York City apartment at 10 West 28th St. was Bob Dylan's home, and I remember everything.
Moving to New York City was a pivotal time for him, and every choice he made then was crucial - the first important crossroad in

his career. Even after he moved out, he would come back to visit, sometimes to get more advice from my parents on the personal issues affecting his life.

My family always protected Bob's privacy, rarely speaking out, and then only with his knowledge. He had his own way of signaling. He knew the answers would be truthful, but just as importantly, discrete. His trust in my parents was limitless. We were intimate observers of his singular talent as he grew from earnest teenager to serious adult. While his stay at 28th St. has been documented, no one else knows how deep the relationship ran, nor what transpired there; the why it was so influential, emotionally and professionally to his development. It is the key missing piece of Bob Dylan history. By all accounts his rise to fame would not have happened as rapidly, or smoothly without the McKenzies.

Bob always looked out for me. If I liked a shirt he was wearing he let me wear it. On many afternoons when he finished his daytime business, he'd take out his guitar and the lessons began. He showed me his music techniques as well as the special way he played harmonica.

"Brownie McGee played this way," he would say. "Jesse Fuller played this way. Now master them and you'll come up with your own style."

No one else got that kind of tutelage from him. If I had a problem with any of my contemporaries, he'd advise me how to handle it. He loved my artwork and always asked me how I got my ideas. We talked about history and literature. I met his fellow musicians when they dropped by the apartment, or when we'd go on outside adventures together. He loved to prank Dave Van Ronk. It was always the real Bob; no pretense of hiding behind a mask, unlike the many other personas he began trying on for public consumption as time and fame progressed.

The first time we met him was February 16, 1961. Three months later he decided the pillows on our couch were where he wanted to rest his head. When he asked my mother to be his foster mother she just smiled. She had a strong feeling his claim to being an orphan was a product of his fertile imagination. Besides, she was already fulfilling that role. And as it turned out he was calling his mother in Minnesota on the sly several times a month.

For those who weren't around or born yet, but have discovered and love his music, New York City was a different kind of place then. It was the hotbed for all things artistic--the place to be. While it can still be an interesting place the ambiance is completely different. It's way more filled with concrete and much more bottom line, business oriented. It doesn't have the same free spirit open to new ideas when a fellow from the Midwest first hit town. In fact, about 15 years after our first contact Bob said to us:

"You know, the way things are now, if I showed up on the scene and tried to break in I might not get in the door."

While sitting one day at 10 W., my back to the sunlit window in the living room, I realized it was almost a lifetime ago since the first morning I woke up in May 1961 (my sophomore year in high school) and saw Bob Dylan sound asleep on our living room couch, blankets askew and hair sticking up. I have always carried that mental snapshot with me. I couldn't wait for the school day to end to see him back home.

I started thinking about then and now. All the who's and what's that used to come in and out of the apartment as if it were a revolving door. My parents, Eve and Mac, were always friendly, hospitable, there to greet everyone and make them feel as if they were at home.

I spoke with Bob right after he hit the five-decade mark.

He said:

"Thirty didn't bother me. Forty was no big deal. But when fifty happened it was time to take stock of my life."

He did look back, after all.

The conversation wasn't entirely serious. He decided to give me some advice on how to pick up women.

"Pete," I'm going to give you some very valuable input. Listen closely and don't forget. I'm going to show you how to get anyone you want. It's foolproof. When you go to a party dress a little off the beaten track, but spiffy. Stand against one of the walls as if you're just observing. It will give off this mysterious aura. Before you know it all the women will be coming over to you because they can't resist mystery. Then make your move."

"Thank you, Bob," I replied. "That's very nice of you to share your knowledge with me. There's only one problem with it."

"What's that?" he asked, deadpan, already anticipating my answer.

"You're Bob Dylan and I'm not."

His laughter on the other end of the phone was immediate. Some things never change in a relationship.

I thought back again to the first morning Bob was asleep on our couch. I was only 15 and he was all of 19. He didn't even look like he had to shave yet. As I speak, both of us are older than my parents were on that May morning. He had shown up, sat himself down, and from that moment the die was cast. His famous poem, "My Life in a Stolen Moment", published in the program of his first solo concert appearance at Town Hall in New York City, April 12, 1963, commemorates this.

Who could possibly dream what the next several decades would bring? Even though I thought he was the greatest thing, the older brother I always wanted (me being an only child), he was there simply because my parents and I loved him... and he loved us. He was himself with that infectious laugh. A broke and talented kid who'd come in from the cold that my parents gave "Shelter from the Storm."

I found myself back in New York City in the middle part a' summer stayin' on 28th
  street with kind, honest, hard workin' people who were good to me—
I got wrote up in the Times after playin' in the fall at Gerde's Folk City—
I got recorded at Columbia after being wrote up in the Times—

("My Life In A Stolen Moment" excerpt from the program.)

P.K.M.

CHAPTER 1: FEBRUARY 16, 1961 – THE FIRST TIME

My parents were out for the evening. Although I was half asleep when the phone rang at 11 p.m. I jumped out of bed and sprinted through the apartment to answer it. It was my mother.

"You have to come down here right now. It's a place called Gerde's Folk City. It's on the corner of 4th St., a couple blocks east of Washington Square Park. You can't miss it."

"How was Jack's concert?" I asked.

My parents had attended a Jack Elliott [1] concert at Carnegie Chapter Hall earlier that evening.

"The concert was fine," she replied. "But you have to come down here now! Jack is here with us and one of your father's oldest friends, Cisco Houston [2], is performing."

I knew who Cisco Houston was. Jack and my dad had told me about him. I'd heard some of his records. He was an old Woody Guthrie traveling companion, like Jack. A big union man with a commanding presence. The name Gerde's Folk City was not familiar to me. I heard glasses clanking and people's voices in the background.

"Jack and your father want to see you," she added.

Something special must be going on for her to be that insistent, so I grabbed the first shirt I could find, put on my khakis, shoes, school jacket, and out the door I went. Got to the subway stop on the corner of 28th Street and Broadway. As I went through the turnstile, the downtown train was pulling into the station. Five minutes later I exited the 8th Street and Broadway stop. It was a bit chilly, but it didn't bother me. A few blocks later, there it was, a big awning with the words "Gerde's Folk City."

As I started through the door, I suddenly realized it was a bar. I was 15 and walking into a place where, if you're under 18, you get stopped at the door, turned around, and ushered right back out on the street. And yes, the minute the front door closed behind me, the bouncer was right there.

"You're a bit young to be here, laddie, don't you think?"

Before I could answer, I noticed a sign that called for a two-drink minimum. I was screwed. Then a voice from somewhere far inside called out:

"He's with me. Let him in!"

It was Jack Elliott.

"No problem, Jack. Go right in," the bouncer said.

I'd never been in a place like this before. It was dark, but nicely laid out. The bar at the back was quite long and lined with stools. There was a roomy aisle to walk back and forth with a 4-foot wooden barrier separating it from the main room. The main room had a whole bunch of tables and chairs. Against its far wall, in the center, was a small, raised stage with a microphone stand. A direct spotlight illuminated it. Off to the side was an old, upright piano. I went over to Jack and shook hands.

"Your folks told me why you couldn't make it. It's okay. School should always come first. I came down right after the concert to see Cisco sing. He's a real old friend. See over there? He's with your dad. They haven't seen each other since World War 2."

My father and Cisco were at the very far end of the bar. I walked over.

"Hi, dad."

"Pete, I'd like you to meet an old friend of mine from the National Maritime Union [3], Cisco Houston."

"Pleased to meet you, young sir," said Cisco, extending his hand. He was strikingly handsome.

"Me, too," I replied. "I've heard a lot about you.

He looked at my father.

"Nice kid you got there, Mac."

I knew my dad's facial expressions pretty well. They could be very subtle. He had the ability, when needed, to maintain a poker face. When he chose to, it was almost impossible to read. When he was young, he'd played cards for a living. As he talked to Cisco I noticed the sadness in my father's eyes. It was only later he told me Cisco was suffering from terminal cancer and had only a short time left. Cisco was a courageous man. He'd survived being torpedoed a couple of times in the War. That courage never left him. You can tell a lot about a man by the way he faces death when it stares him in the eye. I'm sorry we never got a chance to see him again. His music had a big effect on Bob.

"Pete, your mother is in the main room with some people. Why don't you go over there so she'll know you got here okay," my father said.

It was clear he had some personal things to discuss with Cisco, so I said goodbye, waved to Jack, and went to find my mother. She was sitting at a table right inside the divider, far from the stage. I went over to her and sat down. Two other people were there with her. My mother introduced us.

"Peter, I'd like you to meet an old friend of mine, Marjorie Guthrie, and her son, Arlo."

I looked at Arlo [4]. He was a year younger than I and had curly hair like mine.

Marjorie was Woody Guthrie's ex-wife. She lived way out of Manhattan in Howard Beach. Both my mom and Marjorie had been dancers with Martha Graham [5]. Both were wives of prominent names in the American labor movement. I wanted to talk to Arlo, but since the talk between Marjorie and my mother was nonstop, I kept sipping my soda. Then, when it looked like there would be a break in the conversation and I could talk to Arlo, an all-encompassing cloud of cigarette smoke wafted across the table. The smell was extremely pungent. Sandwiches had just arrived at the table. For me, trying to eat something with that smell hovering over the food was impossible. I thought it would pass. However, no sooner had the smoke cleared and I was about to grab a sandwich when another large cloud came floating by.

Now I was pissed. I had gotten to meet Cisco Houston and Woody Guthrie's wife. I was hearing stories about Woody and Cisco and learning things about my father from Marjorie and my mother. I was looking forward to making friends with Arlo. In 1956 Pete Seeger had been my elementary school's visiting music class instructor when I was ten years old in 5th grade there. Everyone was given sheets of paper with the words and music printed on them, and we would have wonderful sing-alongs. Knowing the bond between Pete and Woody I figured Arlo might have some cool stories.

Then that cloud of smoke drifted in, AGAIN. I turned around in my seat to see where that heavy, hanging smell was coming from, and there was the offender. He must have just slipped in and sat down in front while no one was looking. He hardly looked older than me. He was by himself, kind of slouched down, a cap pulled over his forehead, a too big black overcoat, boots, legs crossed, with the crossed leg bobbing like it wanted to go somewhere but couldn't decide which way to go. Out of the corner of my eye I watched as he put out one cigarette and lit another and realized it wasn't going to stop. I wouldn't be able to enjoy my sandwich. I was about to say:

"Would you mind, that smoke is really bothering me. Could you stop, or else move," when I heard Marjorie Guthrie's voice.

"Peter, I see you've noticed our friend. His name is Bob Dylan. He's a young folk singer from New Mexico [6] who just came into New York to visit Woody in the hospital. He even wrote a special song for him. Woody liked it."

That was it. There was nothing I could do now except force a smile and say, "Nice to meet you."

He looked at me and nodded his head slightly, but made no sound. My mother looked at him from across our table. I had been introduced, so it was only proper etiquette she be polite as well.

"Hello," she said.

He nodded again, still without a word. My mother turned back to Marjorie and commented:

"He has such a baby face and he's all alone."

She turned again to look at him in the dim light and saw he was nursing a drink with no food in front of him.

"Have you eaten? You should always have something in your stomach when you drink. The sandwiches on our table came free with the drinks. You have some."

He looked back at her and muttered something. Even though I was closest, it was unintelligible. My mother lifted the full plate of sandwiches, handed it to me and said, "Peter, give this to him."

He nodded once again. After I passed it over I couldn't believe it; I never saw an entire plate of sandwiches disappear so fast - including the one I was going to eat.

Mom and Marjorie resumed talking about old times. It was getting late. Cisco was looking a bit tired, although still engaged in conversation with my father. Marjorie and Arlo had a long trip home. Jack had a few drinks under his belt. It was time to go. I was glad Jack's concert went well. We all said our goodbyes. My parents and I made it out through the swinging doors to the street. I could now feel how much colder it had become. Fortunately, as deserted as the streets in that part of the Village normally were at that time of night, we got lucky and caught a taxi. At that moment God was definitely "On Our Side."

(Cisco Houston)   (Cisco l., Woody Guthrie c., Pete Seeger r.)

(Pete Seeger at my school, DCS. Nan Seldin L., Pete Seeger c., David Lauterbach r.)

CHAPTER 2: THE LUNGS WERE REALLY BLOWN OUT

The second angriest I ever saw Bob Dylan was one night in June 1961. He had been hired to play harmonica on a Harry Belafonte [7] album called "The Midnight Special." He was really excited about it. I didn't know how he got the booking, but he had built up a reputation for his harmonica playing. Not guitar and harmonica, just the harmonica cupped in his hands. Sonny Terry [8], the legendary "harp master" on the blues and folk scene, called Bob "the gosh darnedest white boy harmonica player there was." Bob liked Harry Belafonte's music and was really looking forward to the session. He had told my mother his dream was "that I can become as big as Harry Belafonte."

He was scheduled to play on three songs. He thought he had died and gone to heaven.

Approximately 6:30 pm the night of the recording session he was almost ready to leave our apartment.

My mother saw the harmonicas on the couch.

"Wait a minute, I have something for you," she said.

She exited the room and came back with a little blue pouch with a string attached.

"Here, Bobby. You can put all your harmonicas in there and they'll all be in one place, and you won't misplace any."

"Oh, thanks, Eve."

He put all the harmonicas in the pouch.

"Now let me look at you."

He turned toward her. She adjusted his shirt collar and made sure his jacket sat squarely on his shoulders.

"Perfect," she said and gave him a kiss on the cheek.

Off he went.

We settled in for a quiet evening, looking forward to hearing about everything in the morning. But soon there were heavy stomping noises echoing up the stairs. The front door opened, and much to our surprise there stood Bob. His left arm flicked out and the bag of harmonicas went flying over the lamp atop the little storage chest at the foot of the living room couch. It landed with a clacking jangle next to his sleep pillow. Clearly, something wasn't quite right.

"It's only 10 o'clock", said my mother. "You already finished?"

You could see his spine bristling and his legs jiggling. He was not pleased.

"Those people must be crazy," he replied.

"What do you mean?" asked Dad.

I was quiet.

"Take after take after take. What do they want? I play the song right every time, but they're not satisfied with the whole arrangement. They make a change and say, 'Do it again.' Never ask me to do anything different. I'm doing it right every time. They should have known what they were doing before they started. Must have done the first song a dozen times. I'm half blowed out. Then this guy in the sound booth says 'Good job, we're getting there. Let's try it again.' I didn't sign on for that. I took my harmonicas and left."

"What about the other two songs?" asked Mom.

"Let 'em get someone else!"

He was still pacing, and angry.

"Sit down and relax," said my father. "Pete, get Bobby something to drink. His throat must be dry,"

I got him a glass of water. He sat down on the couch and took a sip. That seemed to break the tension. He was quiet for a moment, shaking his head. Even though it was unheard of for someone to leave a Belafonte recording session, my father reasoned that what Bob did was okay.

"The good thing is that you were able to hold it in until you got home. You didn't create a scene there. To them, for all appearances, all you did was leave. No harm done."

That appeared to diffuse Bob's momentary, internal rumblings even more because he knew my father didn't make empty statements. How my father could be so sure of what he was saying Bob didn't know, but he trusted him. You could see it in his shoulders.

The answer was simple. The next day my father went upstairs to talk with our neighbor, Hank Pearson. Hank just happened to be Mr. Belafonte's old Navy buddy. They had started a food concession business together after World War 2 and had remained close friends. My father told him what had happened. He asked Hank to smooth it over with Belafonte the next time he saw him.

"Yes, of course, Mac. Be glad to."

I don't know if Hank had a chance to do that, but Dad did make the effort. That was the important thing. He never told Bob about it and told me not to say anything about it, either. I didn't... until now.

(Actual harmonica in the key of D used by Bob on the recording)

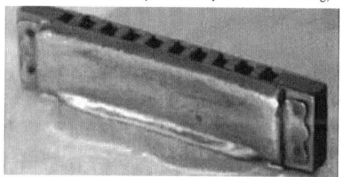

Guitar:	Millard Thomas
Guitar:	Ernie Calabria
Bass:	Norman Keenan
Drums:	Danny Barrajanos
	Don Lamond
	Percy Brice
Trumpet Solos:	Joe Wilder
Saxophone Solos:	Jerome Richardson
Harmonica:	Bob Dylan*
Engineering and Mastering:	Bob Simpson
Photos:	Peter Perri

STEREO SF-5132
(LSP 2449)

SIDE 1

MIDNIGHT SPECIAL (Arr.: Belafonte)

Let the Midnight Special shine its ever-
lovin' light on me

CHAPTER 3: JACK ELLIOTT

In 1961, from May through September, our Manhattan apartment was the best place for Bob Dylan to be. It became his own private space where no one would bother him, and he could work out all his moves. How a hungry, almost 20-year-old arrived at my parent's doorstep, where throwing a bag of harmonicas in anger would get him reassurance, not admonishment, is a story unto itself. It involves a few special individuals, a special street and building. Without that synchronicity it's anyone's guess what alternate reality would now exist but for a very specific chain of events. To know that story within a story you need to hear about certain other people. It won't take long…

My mother and father moved into their apartment after they got married in 1938. They moved there because it was a quiet street, with a subway stop on the corner for transportation. A Chinese laundry was across the street right near a flower shop. A bar was on the N.W. corner of 28th and Broadway. Our building used to have a stoop with stairs, a hat store and a barbershop adjacent to the stoop. It's all changed with time.

The family upstairs on the top floor was black, and originally from South Carolina. They had been in the building almost as long as my parents. They had both apartments and were all wonderful people. In apartment 5R was the aforementioned Hank Pearson and his wife, Frances. Hank's sister, Mommy Dorcas, had the other apartment, 5F, across the hall. Her husband, Frank Neal, was a professional dancer and artist. They had two daughters,

"Little Dorcas" and her younger sister, Sharon. Both girls were a couple of years older than I. The whole building seemed like one big family house. In those days, in New York, you didn't need to keep your front door locked. If you wanted to visit a neighbor you just knocked on the door and walked in. Or, people just left them wide open. It was great in the summertime for cross breezes. We couldn't afford air-conditioning.

(10 W. 28th St.)

Right across the hall from us, in apartment 4F, were Sasha and Frida Maruches and their son, Dick. Dick was a decade older than I. Sasha was from Russia and was a Grandmaster at chess. He would patiently try to teach me how to play the game. As good a student as I was in school, I can't say the same for chess. I knew how to play, but never could concentrate enough on it to be anything more than a beginner. Bob went across the hall several times, later on, to play chess with Sasha; he had a real knack for it.

In mid-1960, Howard Harrison, a 24-year-old aspiring photographer and recent Harvard graduate, moved into an apartment that was on the floor below us. Howard later took one of the most iconic photos of Bob, the one that appears on the cover of Bob's concert program at Carnegie Chapter Hall on November 4, 1961. It's included in the official "BOB DYLAN SCRAPBOOK" (2005).

Bob said:

"I love that photo. It looks like me."

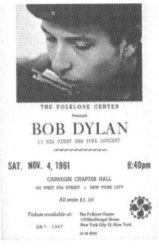

Howard was living with Anne-Marie, his girlfriend at the time. She was a free spirit, one of the original flower children. At first glance she was often mistaken for Joan Baez [9]. When she went down to the Greenwich Village clubs people did double takes. She was very popular among the artists and musicians.

Joan Baez and my mother talked about Anne-Marie on October 31, 1964, at Philharmonic Hall in NYC, the night of Bob's Halloween concert there. My aunt, Gig, and my mother were in the dressing room backstage before the performance. Bob was running back and forth. Gig said:

"Bobby, you have something on your trousers"

He looked down, saw it and brushed it off. It was a piece of lint.
"Thanks," he said.

My mother looked at Joan:

"In person, you and Anne-Marie don't look at all alike."

Joan replied with a roll of the eyes:

"The trouble that girl got me into…"

(Anne-Marie 1961)

Since we didn't have a TV, I would occasionally go downstairs to Howard's to watch a show. On February 8th, 1961, Howard and Anne-Marie were out, and Walt Disney's "Robin Hood" was on. I went downstairs to watch it. I was just learning to play the guitar. While I was watching the movie, the front door to the apartment wide open, there's a light knock and in walks a slim fellow with a cowboy hat and boots.

"Hi, Anne-Marie here?" were the first words out of his mouth in a quiet drawl.

Before I could answer, noticing a guitar in the corner, he asks:

"Hey, is that your guitar?"

"Yes. Why?"

"Do you play it?"

"Yes, I do. You want to hear something?"

"Sure," he replies.

Though I was now missing the movie, I was going to show off my newfound skill. Trying to be nonchalant, I picked up the guitar and went through half my repertoire - 1 three-chord song. I was very proud of myself.

"Not bad," he says. "You know, I play a little myself. Mind if I give it a try?"

His hands flew up and down the fingerboard, playing so many chords and notes I could visually barely keep up. He then stopped.

"What's your name?" he asks.

"Peter McKenzie."

"Nice to meet you, Peter. I'm Jack Elliott."

While the name, Jack Elliott, meant nothing to me at the time, I later learned who he was. Although he was born Elliot Charles Adnopoz in Brooklyn Jack was, and still is, the greatest interpreter of Woody Guthrie's music. Bob used to tease Jack about his real name.

"Adnopoz, Adnopoz," he would laugh.

But, oh were the tables turned when Jack found out that his friend, the high and mighty Bob Dylan, also had a different birth name. He taught Bob a lot.

[Several months later I wound up singing at a party for Jack in a back garden on MacDougal Street. My folks, Bob, Suze Rotolo [10], Dave Van Ronk were all there. I did a song, "San Francisco Bay Blues," Jack was known for. I tried to play it like Jack and sing it like Bob. Both were amused – a kid among the adults.]

"So, where's Anne-Marie?" Jack repeats.

"I don't know and I'm not sure when she'll be back," I answer. "My parents might, though. They're right upstairs in 4R."

"Thanks. Nice guitar playing. See you later," he says.

He went upstairs to see my folks. When he found out who they were it was as if he'd discovered the source. They talked for three hours and hit it off so well Jack invited them to a concert he was giving February 16 at Carnegie Chapter Hall. He never did get to see Anne-Marie that night, but a lasting friendship was made.

(Jack and Woody Guthrie 1950s)

"Nobody can sing Woody like Jack" -From the William Pagel archives-

(Cisco Houston l, Woody Guthrie center at NMU headquarters 1940s)

CHAPTER 4: 1000 MILES FROM HOME

A couple of nights later I was down at Howard's again when a loud voice resonated throughout the apartment:

"Hey, you know where Anne-Marie is?"

"She's out," I automatically replied without looking up.

"Well, she was supposed to be here. I'm Kevin Krown and we were supposed to meet tonight. Who are you?"

"I'm Peter McKenzie."

"So, where's Anne-Marie?"

"I don't know, and I don't know when she's coming back. My parents might, though. They're upstairs. Apartment 4R. You can ask them."

"Thanks, kid."

As I watched his 6'2" skinny frame turn to head upstairs I noticed he had a slight limp. I learned later it was from an old gunshot wound to the hip he received when he was at one of the early sit-ins at segregated diners down South before the freedom rides.

He told my parents he was a friend of Anne-Marie and a freshman at the University of Chicago. They invited him to sit down at the kitchen table. When my father noticed him looking at something atop the mantelpiece over the brick fireplace, he said to him:

"That's a 12-year-old bottle of Scotch up there. Would you like to wet your whistle?"

The bottle was full. My father only drank a half a glass, but by the end of the evening it was empty.

My parents and Kevin talked quite a while. His main academic interests were history and politics. They discussed various aspects of the American labor movement. My father was impressed with his knowledge on the subject, how well read he was and his enormous vocabulary. When Woody Guthrie's name was mentioned, Kevin's eyes lit up.

"I met him."

That piqued my father's interest. How could this 18-year-old from Malverne, Long Island, possibly know Woody Guthrie?

"How so?" he asked.

"I had a folksinger friend staying with me in Chicago. He was chomping at the bit to meet him. We knew Woody was ill and in a hospital in New Jersey. Two weeks ago, we drove from Chicago to New York together. After we arrived, we went out to the hospital to see him. When we were shown into his room my friend sang him a song he had written about him."

[Weeks later when Bob started visiting us on his own, he told us about the experience himself.

"I went to see Woody in the hospital in New Jersey with Kevin and Mark (Eastman) right after we all arrived in New York. All the pictures I had seen of him was this lively, healthy man who was a giant in my eyes. There he was in a bed, kind of shrunken from his disease and it was difficult for him to talk. I took out a guitar and sang him a song I told him I had written just for him. He liked it and I sang some more. It felt good knowing I had made the great man happy."]

I'd already come up from downstairs while they were talking. As they spoke about the Russian Revolution, the Civil War, writers like Dostoevsky, Chekov and Henry Miller, Kevin poured himself another drink.

I listened intently. I never knew my dad read Henry Miller. By the quotes and facts my father seemed to pull out of nowhere was the first time I realized he had a photographic memory.

By the end of the evening Kevin, like Jack Elliott, had bonded with us.

.

(Kevin Krown)

CHAPTER 5: AFTER GERDE'S

After the night of February 16 at Gerde's I figured things would revert to normal. But, after that night, almost every day, I would come home from school to a half empty bottle of Scotch on the kitchen table and Kevin Krown engaged in a conversation with my mother. Not our Scotch. We couldn't afford it. Kevin brought it and drank it while he was waiting for my father to get home. Amazingly, he never seemed inebriated.

One of the reasons Kevin, Jack, and later, Bob, gravitated to our apartment was because of my father's background.

He had been one of the founders and leaders of the National Maritime Union, NMU for short. All the seamen who worked on regular ships, ocean liners, and the Merchant Marine became members. As First Vice President my father was chief negotiator for all union contracts. The NMU was the first integrated union where its black and white members slept in the same quarters during the 1930s and 1940s. During WW2 my father was on the National War Labor Board under Eleanor Roosevelt. They were in charge of providing and overseeing the sailors who worked the Lend-Lease [11] program with England, sending goods on "liberty ships" and other freighters and tankers in a grand effort to help stop the Nazis. Two of the members of the NMU were Woody Guthrie and Cisco Houston. Woody's famous song, "The Sinking of the Reuben James," is about the first American warship, a destroyer escorting a convoy to England, sunk by a Nazi U-Boat.

Woody also wrote a song about the "liberty ships" themselves called "Talking Merchant Marine."

Here's an excerpt:

Ship loaded down with TNT
All out across the rollin' sea;
Stood on the deck, watched the fishes swim,
I'se a-prayin' them fish wasn't made out of tin [12].
Sharks, porpoises, jellybeans, rainbow trouts, mudcats, jugars, all
over that water.
Win some freedom, liberty, stuff like that.

This convoy's the biggest I ever did see,
Stretches all the way out across the sea;
And the ships blow the whistles and a-rang her bells,
Gonna blow them fascists all to hell!

I'm just one of the merchant crew,
I belong to the union called the N. M. U.
I'm a union man from head to toe,
I'm U. S. A. and C. I. O.
Fightin' out here on the waters to win some freedom on the land.

Woody and Cisco would perform songs together at rallies, strikes, and other NMU functions. Pete Seeger [13] would be there as well, with his banjo and members of the Almanac Singers. Jack had been doing "Talking Merchant Marine" for years. Bob also performed it at his first solo concert at Carnegie Chapter Hall in November 1961. Kevin, like Jack, wanted to hear all about it from the source himself.

Kevin had some stories of his own. When he came up with the idea to print the Lord's Prayer on a Lincoln penny, put a little hole in it so it could be worn around the neck and sell it for a dollar all around Chicago, the Feds came in and put a stop to it. I saw one. Another was selling shots of oxygen, again for a dollar, to tired students who had been up all night studying for exams. Who knows what hospital he was getting the tanks from? When the University President got wind of it... end of venture. Then there was an actor Kevin hired to impersonate a no-show politician in a local political debate he had organized at the University of Chicago.

The stories poured out of his head as the Scotch was pouring into his glass. Most were later confirmed as true by several of his classmates who started showing up with him. Then came his girlfriends. Then came their girlfriends. Then some started showing up without him. It seemed like 28th St. was becoming a home-away-from-home for half of the University of Chicago, whose real homes were literally scattered from California to the New York Island. I was getting a college education while still a sophomore in high school.

One of the names that came up during their varied conversations was Paul Robeson [14]. My dad had known him. Mr. Robeson was black, and his intellectual prowess, political activism, outspoken views, and artistic talent made him a giant of a man, the Frederick Douglass [15], or Martin Luther King of his day. He was also an extraordinary athlete. In the original 1936 Broadway production of Showboat, Mr. Robeson with his deep, resonant, baritone voice, made "Ol' Man River" a national sensation.

Later on, Bob got a very detailed history about Paul Robeson from my father. It served as a guide how to walk that very fine line between the personal, political, and artistic. He learned how to expose some part of himself without getting sidetracked by irrelevant gossip while reaching the biggest possible audience. It also served as a roadmap of what not to do. The importance of that lesson may have faded with time, but back then it was something to which an unknown young man's ears paid close attention.

(Leadbelly,[16] Paul Robeson, Cisco Houston. 1946 – 3 of Bob's heroes)

(My father 1940s)

CHAPTER 6: ALL FIVE

At the beginning of March Kevin was sitting at our kitchen table when he mentioned the name Bob Dylan for the first time.

"Oh," my mother exclaimed, "that's the name of the young man we met at Gerde's after Jack's concert."

"Yeah, I remember. He ate my sandwich," I snapped.

Kevin started explaining how they had become friends. In mid-1960 they first met by chance at a club near Denver, Colorado. When the two of them were in NYC, they palled around together at night and would sometimes wind up crashing at the Washington Square Hotel. It was then called The Earle. Later, I found out about the young ladies boisterous Krown from Big East, Malverne, Long Island and quiet, small-town boy, Dylan, had picked up and taken back there with them. Kevin had made it his business to get to know a lot of the local New York performers— Dave Van Ronk, Jack Elliott, Mark Spoelstra, Danny Kalb [17] and others— and introduced Bob to as many as he could that Bob hadn't first met himself.

Like Bob, Kevin wanted to get away from home as soon as possible. His parents, Jack and Sophie, were very left of center politically. Jack was a contractor and builder. No following in his father's footsteps, or local college for Kevin. He wound up at the University of Chicago, 1000 miles from home.

Kevin had a sharp and sarcastic sense of humor. He started playing guitar and doing satiric stand-up when he was a kid. He was doing it when he and Bob first met. Bob was playing at another club and the two happened to meet at the same table at a different, third club after the end of their gigs. He immediately recognized Bob's potential and Bob recognized his. Kevin told him he had a place in Chicago, and if he found himself in the vicinity, he should look him up first thing.

"We'll have a good time," said Kevin.

Bob did just that. At the very beginning of 1961 he arrived in Chicago and stayed with Kevin. Right off the bat Kevin decided to do something with this talented compatriot. It didn't matter that he was a year younger than Bob. Right then Kevin became Bob's first, unofficial manager. He helped get him some bookings around the Chicago area. He also showed him a very old trick of the trade.

It took time, money, and paperwork to copyright a song with the Library of Congress. Kevin explained how to circumvent it.

"First, you type, or write out the lyric. Then you sign it. After that you put it in a sealed envelope and mail it back to yourself. When you receive it you place it, unopened, in a safe spot. The sealed, unopened envelope with the postmark date containing the manuscript affords the same protection as the L.O.C. copyright. Simple!"

Bob seized on his trick with one of his first famous compositions. The myth of its creation notwithstanding, "Song to Woody" was not originally written on February 14, 1961, at Mills Tavern in NYC. Bob wrote it in early January 1961 while in Chicago with Kevin. It was typed with handwritten corrections, put in a sealed envelope, then mailed back to himself c/o Kevin Krown at Kevin's Chicago address before Bob came to New York. The manuscript now resides in the permanent collection of the Morgan Library in New York City. An image of it appears in "No Direction Home,"

Martin Scorsese's four-hour documentary on Bob made in conjunction with the Dylan organization. Bob's voice can be heard in the background on the soundtrack.

(Bob's original typed manuscript with handwritten corrections-1961)

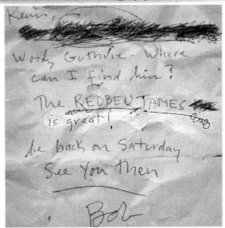

(Note from Bob to Kevin when Bob was with him in Chicago-1961)
-From the William Pagel archives-

With the "poor man's" version of the lyric copyright in the mail, it was time to take a leap. In late January 1961 Bob, Kevin, Mark Eastman, and one other, took off for New York City and then to Greystone Hospital in New Jersey to see Woody Guthrie.

As exciting as that visit to Woody turned out to be, Bob still needed a place to stay. Kevin had his toasty-warm parents' house on Long Island to go back to every night. They hadn't thought about where Bob would stay before leaving Chicago. Kevin couldn't just bring him home with him. Fortunately, Kevin had friends in the city who had no problem putting Bob up for few days while Kevin got the ok for him to stay at his parents' home. They could find more permanent digs for him later. As soon as Bob was ensconced in Kevin's house, he started listening to his New York record collection, just like in Chicago.

IMPORTANT!
REFERENCE NOTES

A booklet with authoritative material is yours free of charge with this album. If you did not receive it, simply fill in this card and drop it in the mailbox.

Name Bob Dylan c/o Kevin Krown

Address -56 Lawrence Ave. Malverne NY

Name and Number of Album Darling Corey # 2003

Remarks -Send booklet

(Card sent by Bob from Kevin's house)

Kevin had two sisters. The younger one, Cathy, living at home, liked it when Bob's new city friends trekked out there to visit. Her favorite was John Cohen of The New Lost City Ramblers [18].

At the same time Bob befriended Sid and Bob Gleason in New Jersey. They were nice people and friends of Woody Guthrie. It was easy for him to get from their house to Greystone Hospital where Woody was. Kevin would swing by there as well.

The Gleasons had a tape recorder. They would bring it out and

Kevin would help record Bob, experimenting to find the best way to sing into a microphone. They finally got six songs on tape they both liked. Kevin started sending copies around to record companies. All turned him down. Some later claimed they were eager to sign Bob, but "that someone else got their bid in first."

One of the places Bob stayed at next was the home of Camilla Adams, an older lady who lived just off Washington Square in Greenwich Village. She was working at Izzy Young's, The Folklore Center. She liked Bob when he first came in and offered him a place to sleep in a room at the back of the store. He soon became a guest for a short time in her apartment.

At the end of the first week in March Anne-Marie threw an open house downstairs at 10 West. There were guitars here, harmonicas there, food in the kitchen, liquor in the cabinets. Kevin, who'd spent part of the day downstairs with Anne-Marie, was sitting in our living room with Mom and Dad talking about an old friend of my father's, Harry Bridges [19], head of the International Longshoreman's Association on the West Coast.

Suddenly, Kevin says, "Eve, Mac, let's go downstairs and see what's going on."

As I get up, he tells me, "Pete, you can come another time. You have to do your homework. The world has big plans for you."

That didn't please me at all. Who was he to tell me what I could or couldn't do?

"Peter, he's right. Schoolwork comes first," my mother said.

There it was. I was staying upstairs, and Kevin and my folks were going to a party and have fun. But that didn't stop me from listening in. When they went downstairs, I cracked open our front door. I could hear the raucous singing and playing and a few bits and pieces of conversations that occurred in the hallway. I did my homework on the train riding up to school the next morning.

The next afternoon Kevin dropped by the apartment in a sunny mood.

"You like the party, Eve?"

"Yes, Kevin. You know," she said, "you really do have an eye for talent."

While my parents were downstairs with the musicians, guitars, food scattered all over, guys ogling Anne-Marie, and any other girls that were there, Kevin had asked my mother of all the people present, if she had to pick one, who she thought had that special something? My mother looked around the room at all the various guitar strummers, vocal hummers and just plain bummers. She pointed her finger at a young man off in the corner, with tousled hair, sitting on the floor playing a brown guitar.

"That one. That's the one to watch.

The following day, after school, Kevin showed up with a friend. It was the fellow my mother had pointed out two evenings earlier.

"Eve," he said, "this is Bob Dylan. Bob, this is Eve McKenzie... and her son, Peter."

"Yes, I remember you," remarked my mother. "You're the young man Marjorie introduced to us at Gerde's. You had a hat on, and you were hungry. I saw you the other night while you were playing your guitar at Howard's and told Kevin I thought you had something special."

He shifted silently in place but said nothing in response to the unexpected compliment.

"Sandwich thief," I thought to myself.

"Well, fellas, make yourself at home. Hungry?" she asked.

A chuckle came from Bob, never one to refuse food placed in front of him. Kevin, despite my disagreement with him about attending the party, I had already come to really like in the short time I had known him. Despite my first impression of him at

Gerde's, this fellow, Bob, had an aura about him that started to intrigue me. It was something about the different kind of depth I could sense in the motion of his eyes.

When Dad got home a short time later the real talk started; the old west, Woody Guthrie, labor history, current politics. Bob was already casting an eye on our record collection, which consisted mostly of old 78s. He was observing as much of the apartment as he could.

There we were, Kevin, Bob, my mother, my father and I, in the same room for the first time.

The evening went reasonably well. Kevin did almost all the talking. He and Bob were like a well-rehearsed vaudeville act. Kevin would talk; when he stopped to take a breath, Bob would throw in a sentence or two to bridge the gap. Finally, he had uttered more than a grunt. Mostly he listened, sizing up the situation. He seemed to like what he saw, because from that day he, too, started dropping by on a regular basis, with or without Kevin. It turned out he could talk a blue streak when he wanted. At first, when he talked about the guitar, most of it was a bit above my experience level. Poor fellow! He didn't know what was about to hit him. I peppered him with questions.

"Bobby, how do you play that chord? How do you get that damping sound? How do you play that rhythm?"

Patiently, he even gave me pointers about my homework, particularly my essays. Truth be told, in private, Bob had a perfect command of the English language; his grammar was impeccable. On stage it was purposely another story.

Whenever he showed up it made me feel good, as if I were being let in on a big secret just the two of us shared... a bonding of two young people: two teenagers, one older, one younger.

(Me at 15 playing the guitar)

CHAPTER 7: APRIL 11, 1961 – OPENING NIGHT

Bob came through the front door all excited.

"I got a girl, I got a girl," he announced.

There he was, like a big school kid. It was late March.

"You gotta meet her."

"Of course," Mom and Dad replied. "Bring her over."

What a young lady she was! Her name was Avril Weber. She was an artist and dancer from San Francisco who had met Bob one night at Gerde's. They'd struck up a conversation and hit it off. I developed an immediate teenage crush. She was sweet, smart, pretty, and an incredible artist. My folks liked her immediately. So did Kevin, Anne-Marie and Howard. Everyone liked her.

Bob kept making the rounds to all the local clubs befriending everyone, from performers to club owners. Mike Porco of Gerde's Folk City was his favorite. Gerde's was the premier folk club in New York. Bob was so engaging because he could talk about any subject on the planet. What he didn't know he could invent. By the end of the conversation, you would think he knew all about it. On the other hand, when he wanted, he could make someone think he was the dumbest hick that ever fell off the turnip truck. That disarmed people making it easier for him to access their little "tricks" without them catching on. Kevin was the same way.

Word of Bob was getting around. Terri Thal, Dave Van Ronk's wife, was working on getting him noticed. Dave was also known as the "Mayor of MacDougal Street," the same title as his later acclaimed memoir. He was a great singer and guitarist. Blues and jazz mostly. He was a little older and took a shine to Bob. Then, at the beginning of April, Bob came running into our living room.

"I got a two-week paying job at Gerde's playing on the same bill with John Lee Hooker (20)."

He was getting more animated with each word.

We were all thrilled. Technically, Bob was underage. Legally a performer had to be 21, or have an official guardian, to get a Musicians' Union card and get paid to perform in a club where liquor was sold. He was still 19.

Since the beginning, the mechanics of how this issue was finessed have been a little murky. Mike Porco, the owner of Gerde's, did claim on Bob's Musician's Union application that he was Bob's legal guardian. What no one knows when he went up their headquarters to get his card he was accompanied by Jack Elliott. While no one would normally question the validity of Mr. Porco's assertion, it certainly didn't hurt to have Jack with him for insurance. As the two of them left, he proudly showed Jack his bright, newly minted card with his name on it. He could now play anywhere and get paid.

Mike Porco was a terrific fellow. With a wonderful, friendly demeanor, he loved what he did. He loved performers, but he especially loved Bob. He was like a father to him.

Every Monday Gerde's had an open microphone night. Anyone who wanted could sign up to do a 15-minute set for free, hoping to either get discovered, or just try out new material. Bob did it often. There were musicians, writers, poets, comedians... all on the same night.

Almost from the time he arrived in New York Gerde's had

become like a second home for Bob. He played at other coffee houses, passing the basket around. He played at the Gaslight. He hung out a lot at the Folklore Center with Izzy Young. Izzy was the owner, and a contributing editor at the folk magazine, "Sing Out." His store on Bleecker Street was a place musicians would go to trade stories. The public would come in to buy instruments, or books on folk music. It was a major social hub.

Having become a fixture at Gerde's Bob, if he were hungry, would often be given a meal on the house from Mike. One of the things Bob used to do there was sit on the sidelines when others were performing and start playing along with them on the old upright piano near the stage. No one complained. He had a unique piano style. John Lee loved it. So did Jack Elliott. Many times, when Jack was onstage, he would see Bob and say:

"Help me out, Bob. Get over to the piano and hit the keys."

The afternoon he told us he was going to get paid for being on the same bill with the great John Lee Hooker beginning April 11th, he was walking on air. John Lee had said he liked Bob's rhythm and timing and, for a white boy, "He sure knew how to play the blues."

"What songs do you think I should sing the first night?" Bob asked my parents.

"Bobby, you know better first-hand what you are doing. Trust your instincts. You've got good ones."

He always welcomed their input even though they were the generation he was supposed to be rebelling against. They, in turn, always respected his opinion, never preaching, or looking down on him. They understood he was a young man with a dream who was trying to figure out how to accomplish it. Put another way, when he wrote "The Times They Are A Changin'" a couple of years later, the verse:

"Come mothers and fathers throughout the land
And don't criticize what you can't understand,"

didn't apply to them.

Bob sat down with Kevin and discussed which songs would be best and the order to perform them. I heard some of the conversations while they were both at our apartment. Bob knew so many songs. The statement he made over the years is true:

"All I had to do was hear a song once or twice and I knew how to play and sing it."

I saw it happen, in person, when he would listen to a record.

To me it didn't matter what he chose to sing. I thought everything he did was great.

April 11th finally arrived. It was almost evening. Opening night was just a couple of hours away. Bob had already popped in our apartment earlier and was now downstairs with Anne- Marie. He kept saying:

"I'm playing with John Lee Hooker. He's the man."

John Lee really liked Bob's hand control over fingerpicking, his syncopation, and his interpretation of all southern blues styles. On the guitar, it's not how many notes you can play in a minute, but the notes you don't play. The quality of those you do makes a great guitar player. Bob, when he wanted, could play straight up with the best of them. I recently looked up Rolling Stone's list of the top 100 greatest guitarists of all time. John Lee Hooker's name was on it, as it should be. Whoever put together that list made a big mistake because Bob Dylan's name was not there. Perhaps it's because he is known for his words that no one understands his guitar abilities. When it comes to rhythm - lead guitar, no one was more talented than Bob. Very few on that list could come close to his integrated, solo, technical, music artistry timing, combining guitar and vocals the way he did on his first four albums; the simplicity or complexity of the rhythms and notes he used to back up and complement his voice. If you go back and listen carefully to his guitar playing on his first four albums, from songs like "You're No Good" and "God on Our Side," no one plays the guitar like that. For the better part of six months, I watched him create arrangements and special tunings for his songs.

Anne-Marie was not about to let Bob go on stage with only adrenalin to give him energy. She was making a special chicken dinner for him downstairs while he warmed up on the guitar. He had not yet taken to always wearing his famous cap on stage.

Dinner was almost ready. Bob inspected his harmonicas to make sure they were all okay, checked his harmonica holder and made sure his strings were in good order, though not necessarily in perfect tune.

Sometimes, one of the tactics he used on stage was to pretend his guitar, with his guitar strings at the head of the guitar sticking out every which way instead of being neatly cut, was out of tune. He would spend what seemed like an eternity trying to tune the strings while uttering throwaway comments to the audience. It got them on his side even before he started playing. The first thing the audience would see was a slightly disorganized young man, guitar strings pointing every which way, trying to get himself together while they shared his predicament. Perhaps they anticipated the worst. Then, when he finally finished fiddling around and started to work the guitar and harmonica, he would blow them away. After his apparent bumbling antics, they didn't expect what he was capable of.

When Anne-Marie told him it was time to eat he packed everything up neatly. He put the harmonicas in the compartment inside the guitar case, the harmonica holder flat on the inside bottom of the case, the guitar with the capo over that, then snapped the case shut. He went over to the table and chowed down every bit of food Anne-Marie put in front of him. He washed and dried his hands and hiked up his pants. He put on his jacket and got a good luck kiss from Anne-Marie. He picked up the guitar case and exited the door. He walked the short hallway then turned and went down the two flights of stairs to the street and out of sight.

Bob didn't stop back at 28th street that night, but he was nicely received, and John Lee treated him well.

(Bob Dylan opening night at Gerde's – April 11, 1961)

CHAPTER 8: APRIL 21, 1961

Ten days into his first paying engagement at Gerde's Folk City, about 7 pm, Bob bounced up the stairs to our apartment. In his hand was his prized copy of Woody Guthrie's "Bound for Glory" that he carried with him everywhere he went.

"Have you read it, Eve?" he said to my mother. "You have to read it. It's a real revelation about life."

He had already talked to my father about Woody's union days and listened to all Woody's records. He knew most of Woody's songs. My mother thought his enthusiasm was wonderful. She was always happy when a young person showed such passion. She had lived through the Great Depression that Woody wrote about. My father's actual experiences, though, were a bit closer to what Woody described.

I could see Bob was really kicking up a fuss about the book.

"You have to read it, Eve," he repeated.

But, there was something else at work. The hype about the book had more to do with me than my mother. Being so good at sizing things up he knew my parents, for their own reasons, had always tried to shield me from their personal experiences in those years— the McCarthy witch hunts (21), the union busting, the pain they went through—because of their moral and political beliefs. In the 1940's my mother used to stand at the apartment door holding a baseball bat when my father came up the stairs at night in case anyone was following, or laying in wait to attack him. Since I was a kid, I had known that goons hired by people who wanted to weaken and destroy the National Maritime Union tried to murder him at least twice. Snippets of facts and stories had come up piecemeal over the years, but my parents had never laid out the whole thing. I will never forget the look on Bob's face when they told him some of the stories. His eyes got wide, and his body shifted forward. He said nothing; he was doing his best to absorb the information.

Bob felt I should know my whole legacy, but he knew he couldn't interfere. Even though he already had an adoring, captive audience in me, he was too smart to sabotage my folks' authority directly. His agenda was different. He kept going on and on about the book, knowing my mother would never read it. Still, he insisted, "If you get the chance, Eve. Just in case. I want you to have it."

When Bob decided to be persistent it was impossible to say "No." He took that well-read copy of "Bound for Glory," opened it to the inside front cover, dated it, signed it—April 21,1961, Bob Dylan—and handed it to my mother.

"Thank you, Bobby," she said, kissing him on the cheek.

He knew the moment he left I would be all over it, going through page by page as fast as I could. And that is exactly what happened. As soon as he departed the book found its way into my excited, 15-year-old hands…

Inside were Bob's little scribblings and notations throughout. He had kept it in excellent condition. I thought the book was terrific; not sure if that was because of the way it was written, or because he had owned it. Either way, the desired outcome was achieved.

An image of the inscribed book is featured in the acclaimed "BOB DYLAN SCRAPBOOK 1956-1966."

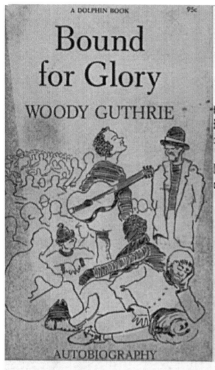

A DOLPHIN BOOK   95¢

Bound for Glory

WOODY GUTHRIE

AUTOBIOGRAPHY

April 21, 1961
Bob Dylan

BOUND FOR GLORY

t no uncle what owns no motorsickle!"
ll"

etful of good rocks and sailed them into

ll Say gone! Who's a liar? I hadda uncle
did! But—but—"

I ain't got no home
I'm ramblin' through this world
Lookin' for a train to ride
Courtin' wide eyed girls

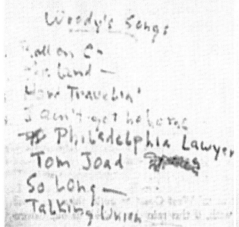

Woody's Songs

"Roll on C"
"his land —
Hard Travelin'
I ain't got no home
Philadelphia Lawyer
Tom Joad
So Long —
Talking Union

1. — got out of —
2. — met a truck —
3. That truck —
4. He found his mothers —
5. — walked down to —
6. Now the twelve —
7. They fed —
8. They stood on the mountain —
9. The Joads rolled away —
10. Now the deputy sheriff —
11. They handcuffed Casey —
12. I prayed to the Lord —
13. Now the deputies come —
14. — grabbed that deputy's club —
15. Tom run back —
16. Everybody might be —
17. Wherever children —

CHAPTER 9: THE COUCH

Bob's two-week engagement at Gerde's passed very quickly. My friends wondered why I was talking so much about this "Bobby" guy. What was the big deal, anyway? They did notice, though, a marked improvement in my guitar playing. They were curious about the "different" style.

As soon as his Gerde's gig ended, Bob took off out of town. It appeared things around the McKenzie household would be slowing down for a bit...

To this day it still amazes me how Kevin could convince almost anyone there was no other option to a scenario than the one he laid out. A week after Bob took off, he told my mother:

"Eve, Bobby was staying at Avril's place. Now that he's gone, she's afraid to be there alone at night. You know what a nice girl she is. Since he's going to be away for a little while, is it okay if she drops by herself to say 'hello'?"

"Of course," was the reply.

The very next day Avril stops in.

"He's gone," she exclaims. "He just picked himself up and left. I didn't know that he wasn't coming right back. Can I come and stay here a little while? I'm afraid to go back to my studio. I don't want to be alone."

This wasn't exactly how Kevin first described it. "Drop by" and "stay" are two different things. But, the groundwork had been laid. He knew my parents' soft spot. They both agreed she could stay until Bob returned.

I thought it was a great idea... Between Bob and Kevin, it seemed like I was slowly acquiring two older brothers. Now, with Avril and Anne-Marie, I was also going to have two more as sisters. I went from being an only child to the youngest of several, just like that. It was fine with me.

With her big brown eyes and a warm smile Avril moved in. A bit shy, but full of energy, she was never shy about helping with the housework, or cooking. She would go down to the Village at night, sometimes with Anne-Marie, and hang out with other artists or Bob's friends. Even when she didn't voice it, you could see she really missed him. In private chats with my mother, she told her things about Bob that would come in handy later when he realized my mother knew more of his true background. Mom never let on, though, or challenged some of the outlandish stories he would tell her about his upbringing and adventures. He appreciated my mother's attitude. It reassured him that she knew exactly what he was up to and why. It was as if they had an unspoken pact. Avril also enjoyed talking with my father about the San Francisco Bay Area. He had spent time there when he'd been Avril's age. She made beautiful pastels for us. Even though my parents are no longer alive, I still have them.

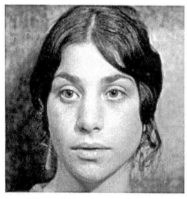
(Avril – photo by Eric Weber)

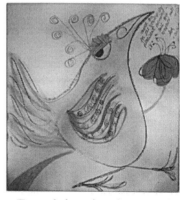
(Pastel drawing by Avril)

Then, suddenly, she received some sort of telegram. Something had happened with her mother in San Francisco.

"I have to leave and go back home," was all she said.

We hadn't heard from Bob since he had left town. She wanted to see him before leaving. But, how were we going to find him?

Fortunately, Kevin Krown was a human antenna when it came to Bob. No matter where, or when he disappeared, Kevin somehow knew where Bob was.

My mother told him, "Kevin, we don't know where Bobby is, and Avril's upset."

In his smooth, swaggering manner he said, "All right, Eve. I'll make a few phone calls." Three calls later Kevin announced, "Bobby's in Wisconsin. He's about to come back to New York."

He told Bob that Avril had to leave shortly for San Francisco because of a family emergency. It was mid-May, but when the time came for Avril to say goodbye, Bob still hadn't shown up.

Although she'd only been with us ten days, I, for one, was going to miss her. When Kevin realized Bob wasn't going to make it back before she left, he tried to coordinate a rendezvous for them in Chicago: Bob on his way back from Wisconsin and Avril on her way out to San Francisco. It didn't pan out.

About 10 pm, a couple days after Avril departed, there was a loud knock on our front door. My mother opened it. Standing in the doorway, a guitar in a black chipboard case in one hand and a small suitcase containing only a single pair of underwear in the other, was Bob.

"Here I am," were the first words out of his mouth.

He was wearing jeans, his usual suede boots, a jacket and a black and yellow checkered shirt. I loved that shirt and eventually commandeered it from him. His hair was a little windblown. He walked in and sat down in the middle of the living room couch.

"Avril still here?"

"No, Bobby, you missed her. She left for San Francisco," my mother said.

"Mmm...," he mumbled.

"You must be hungry."

He smiled... Then she scolded him.

"Bobby, we were worried about you. Avril was worried about you. Why didn't you call to let us know where you were?"

"Ah, you know, Eve, I met some new people and just lost track of time."

The answer wasn't satisfactory for her, but when she saw his sheepish grin, she knew it would have to suffice. They talked back-and-forth and then it was midnight, past my bedtime. I had already opened his guitar case and was toying with the strings.

I said, "Good night," carefully putting the guitar back in the case. They continued talking. Slowly, the sound of voices faded as my eyelids closed and I drifted off.

The next morning, I woke up about 7 am. It usually took about an hour to get ready for school; washing up, getting dressed, gathering the books, eating breakfast. I passed my mom, who was already up, on the way to the bathroom. The bathroom was off to the side of the ten-foot hallway connecting the kitchen and the living room. You could see clearly into the living room before you entered the bathroom. A shape was on the couch with a blanket over it. I was back in the kitchen in a flash.

"Mom, what's going on?"

"Well, Pete, your dad and I were talking with Bobby until 2 am and it was time for us to go to bed. We asked him where he was going to stay, seeing how late it was."

"Don't worry, Eve, I'll find a place."

"You certainly won't be going anywhere, young man," she said.

"It's 2 o'clock in the morning and it's too dangerous to be walking around. Tonight, you sleep here."

I was thrilled. As much as I liked school and hanging out with my friends, I couldn't wait for the day to end so I could hightail it home. That day at school, even my closest friends thought I had finally lost it talking about this "Bobby" guy. A year later they were asking, "Can we come over and visit when he's there?"

As soon as my last class ended, I got in the subway uptown and got out downtown. I covered the few blocks to the house and rushed up the flights of stairs. Bob and Mom were sitting at the kitchen table.

"Hi, Pete."

"Hi, Bobby," I said as I put down my books and sat at the table with them.

"How did school go today?" He asked.

"Are you staying?"

"Now let Bobby be", said my mother. "He's got to go out soon and do a few things."

"What kind of things?"

"Oh, just to meet some people. I'll be back later, and I'll see you then," he assured me.

"Time for your homework," Mom said. I went to my room, closed the door, and started on my homework. I was called out for dinner, but Bob hadn't returned. When it was time for me to go to bed and no Bob, I was very disappointed.

Sometime, in the middle of the night, in a sleepy haze, I heard noises in the kitchen. A few hours later, when I left for school at 8 am, there was Bob with a blanket covering him, sound asleep on the couch, his boots neatly placed on the floor.

CHAPTER **10**:
TIME FOR BREAKFAST

My mother and Bob developed a regular morning routine. He would get out of bed, usually around noon, tousle his hair, put on a pair of pants and a shirt. He accumulated a few more items of clothing, some coming from Dad's closet, which Mom offered him. He didn't have to ask. He would walk to the bathroom, wash his hands and face, and (contrary to legend) brush his teeth, go into the kitchen and light a cigarette as he sat down at the table for breakfast. My mother usually made him eggs, toast and coffee, but he never went to the refrigerator on his own even though he was treated as a member of the family with all family privileges. He was the perfect houseguest, gracious and well mannered.

Over breakfast, he and Mom would talk about the previous night's events—what he did, who he'd met, the kind of friends he was making. That morning ritual was probably the most relaxing part of Bob's day. If he were still around when I got home after school, the poor fellow couldn't get away from me. I tailed around after him, peppering him with "Bobby" this and "Bobby" that, but he took it all in stride.

The family dynamic would define the relationship that Bob had with my mother. He dropped by late one afternoon a couple of years later, in mid-1963, right before I left for college. After saying goodbye, we were standing on our landing as Bob hopped down the stairs. As he reached the landing below, my mother called out to him.

"Bobby, I'm concerned. I know from being in show business with musicians and actors that things like marijuana and other items eventually show up. You have to be careful."

He stopped on a dime, turned around, and in his calmest, most serious voice said, "Eve, you know me. I would never get into that."

"You promise?" she said.

"Aw, c'mon. Why would I?" He looked up and smiled reassuringly.

That was good enough for my mother. One flash of those big, blue doe eyes and the issue was settled then and there. No shortage of information—and misinformation—has circulated about Bob Dylan's drug use over the years, but that never entered into our relationship. Although I lived through the 60's I didn't experiment with drugs. Even as a kid I never took anything more than a box of chocolate donuts washed down with a bottle of soda. Then, again, you could say I had a sugar addiction. Bob learned that I never used drugs when he visited some years later. He let me know he was pleased about it.

So, Mom and Bob would sit in the morning, chatting away. He talked a lot, and she enjoyed the repartee. It took a while, but eventually, Bob revealed that he really came from Duluth via Hibbing, finally putting to rest all the after stories of his times with traveling circuses, riding the rails in box cars, playing music honky-tonks with this or that legend, being raised in an orphanage until he ran away and met Kevin. My parents knew those stories were just that, foundations for a character, or public persona he was creating. He'd tell those stories as a kind of long dress rehearsal, practicing until he got the backstory just right. They knew he'd reveal his real history when he was ready.

One morning he told her a story about going on a wild trip with some friends down south then back to New York. They ran out of gas at one point and one of them had to wire home for money. That's when things got interesting. While waiting for the money, they went up to this mansion, were invited inside, and sat down to eat. The hosts had laid out lots of fancy plates and utensils, but there was nothing on the plates. The part about the empty plates with no food on the table found its way into a line from "Talking New York," a song on his first album:

> A lot of people don't have much food on their table
> But they got a lot of forks 'n' knives
> And they gotta cut somethin'

On another morning they were talking about different musical eras. Bob asked Mom, "Why don't you think I should sing songs from the 30's?"

My mother answered:

"Because it's not your era. Sing your era. You don't want to do what the rest of the folksingers are doing. What does a box car even mean to them?"

Like many other curious young people who had read "Bound for Glory," Bob seemed to have a romanticized vision of hopping on a freight car and riding the rails the way Woody had described it. She wanted to set Bob straight about some of his youthful notions.

"What's so great about riding box cars? Those people who came out of the dust bowl didn't have anything to eat. They had to get a ride any way they could to look for work. It wasn't pleasant. They didn't do it for fun."

When he tried to change topics saying, "I'm thinking of going to San Francisco," she gave him a stern look.

"Are you going by box car, or taking a passenger train?"

He hesitated a moment, searching her face.

"By passenger train," he said, laughing.

My mother never did read the copy of "Bound for Glory" Bob gave her, but my father had actually ridden the rails during the Great Depression. He had been raised in an orphanage till he was five, never knowing who his mother was. After that, his paternal aunt and grandmother raised him in Virginia City, Nevada. At nineteen he left the University of Nevada and headed out for San Francisco, not looking back.

As for me, I finally had the real live in older brother I'd always dreamed of. Bob obliged by really treating me like his kid sibling. Whenever we were both home I'd pepper him with questions about what he did that day. Then I'd pester him to teach me something new on the guitar. Bob knew a seemingly endless amount of guitar stuff. He liked to get a rise out of me by playing as fast as possible so I couldn't quite follow his fingering. He would then play a little slower, but not quite slow enough. Finally, when he'd had his fun, he would slow down enough that I could see what he was doing. I may be one of the few, lucky people for whom he ever opened up his bag of guitar tricks. He was very patient and generous with his time. Take, for example, the way Bob held his hands when fingerpicking. I've never seen anyone position their picking fingers and whole hand around the sound hole on the guitar the way he did. Every other guitar player I've seen holds his arm and hand in a similar way so that the picking fingers are roughly perpendicular to the strings. Bob brought his arm in from the side, so that his thumb and fingers appeared almost parallel to the strings. You have to look at early pictures to see his unique style. His fingers seem to move independently, and his wrist doesn't appear to bend. Between the hand position and the control of his individual fingers, Bob played in an unmistakable style that combined a thumping, driving rhythm with simultaneous note patterns and chording. I have never seen anyone else position and move their fingers in that way. No matter how unique and individual a guitarist's hand positioning and plucking, they all have certain, identifiable similarities. Bob's hands are a completely different animal.

I was now learning art by day and music at night.

I also started to try the harmonica. Bob showed me how he played—sucking in, blowing out, the way he used the tongue on the reeds. My initial attempts sounded God-awful. He tried hard to keep a straight face but couldn't help cracking up. He wasn't laughing at me, though. He was very encouraging. He was just tickled by the serious look on my face. The funny thing was that my father also played the harmonica, and had perfect pitch. He could play any tune after hearing it once. He played in a more traditional style—a straight melody with some vibrato thrown in, like a lone cowboy sitting around a campfire at night. Sometimes he and Bob sat around and played together. Despite the example my father set, I never had any interest in the harmonica until Bob showed up.

I practiced away, mostly when Bob was out of the house. He always made sure to leave plenty of harmonicas around. One day he showed me a particular blues progression, and somehow, I played it back correctly. That time, Bob didn't laugh. He smiled, sat back looking at me for a moment. I could tell by that look he was trying to decide something.

"It's time for the next step," he said, taking out his harmonica rig.

The harmonica rig is the contraption worn around the neck that holds the harmonica so you can play it the same time as the guitar.

"Try it. I can't teach you how to coordinate it. That's something you'll have to learn on your own."

I picked up the guitar, put his rig around my neck, and put in a harmonica in the key of C. I thought that the easiest key to play in since it was a simple and common key for folk guitar, and because that was the key to the harmonica, he had given me.

"Go at it," he said.

I did, setting off another round of laughing and giggling. I couldn't blame him. As awful as my first attempts at the harmonica on its own had sounded, it was nothing compared to the racket I made with the guitar and harmonica together.

"How the heck do you do this?" I protested. I couldn't coordinate anything.

"Pete, all I can say is practice. I can't help you anymore with that," he repeated. "Use the rig whenever you want. You'll get it eventually."

He was right. It took a while, but I did finally get it, and it was fun to do. I eventually got good enough on the harmonica itself that I could teach my high school friend, Peter Blankfield, how to play the way Bob taught me. Years later, when he became known as Peter Wolf, front man for the J. Geils Band, he told me, "You know, you were my musical inspiration."

While that was a wonderful compliment, always Bob was really the root of that inspiration.

(Me playing guitar and harmonica -1962)

CHAPTER 11: FIFTY CENTS A DAY

One thing my parents did from the very beginning was put 50 cents on the living room desk for Bob each morning. That way he always had enough for bus, or train fare and something to eat when he was out and about. Back then fares were only 15 cents. By those days' standards, considering my parent's income, 50 cents was a fair piece of change. I mention the 50 cents because it came up in an incident that happened 30 years later.

In 1991 I was on the phone with Bob. He was out in California. We were discussing the possible sale of the lyrics he had written while living with us my mother had saved. Dad had passed away 11 years earlier. Mom wasn't doing well health wise, and we needed some money for her care. As we always did beforehand in any manner pertaining to Bob, I asked him if it was okay to sell some of the lyrics.

"It's fine with me," he said. "We have to get money for your Ma. I'm going to reach out and put someone in touch with you who deals with this kind of thing and can tell you the best way to do it."

We got into a further discussion about relatives and money, and it became clear he was uncomfortable with family members seeking handouts.

"Pete, there is always some relative somewhere that shows up and thinks it's all right because they consider themselves family to request money."

"You know that's not what I'm asking," I replied.

"Good," he answered.

The manuscripts in question had remained in a drawer at my parents' apartment for 30 years. We didn't want to part with them, but it was out of necessity.

"It'll work out," he said. "I don't understand, though, what all the fuss is about. They're just pieces of paper. Paper isn't worth much."

From his point of view, I could see the logic. To others... well, I'd recently been informed that to collectors and scholars original documents were like diamonds, particularly those of someone with Bob Dylan's stature.

"Wait by the phone. You'll be getting a call soon," he said before we both hung up.

Sotheby's, N.Y., had expressed great interest in auctioning the pieces. I had no idea until then what monetary value these items might have. The professional world of collecting was foreign to me.

The next day I waited by the phone and, sure enough, it rang. Bob had kept his word. It was the man who was supposed to help us with the best way of dealing with the lyrics. His name was Mr. Q (not his real name for legal reasons). He was a lawyer who handled some matters for Bob. He also represented George Harrison and Frank Sinatra.

"What can I do for you?" he asked.

I thought it an odd opening question considering my previous conversation with Bob and the tone of his voice. I responded:

"Do you know who we are?"

"No, but Mr. Dylan asked me to call you."

Ok, I reasoned, little oversights can happen. I took some time and explained the relationship. Then I told him about the lyrics. His response was not what I anticipated.

"What makes you think you have the right to do anything at all with those lyrics?

"What do you mean?"

He went on:

"There are a lot of legal issues regarding copyright and ownership that need to be addressed. My suggestion is that you send me a copy of the manuscripts and then I'll investigate the matter of their sale. Mr. Dylan already has a publisher for his lyrics, and they need to give their approval. If they do get sold, we may be able to work out a percentage arrangement."

This line of reasoning caught me off guard. Like a lawyer, he was looking to maximize the amount of revenue he could generate for his client. I don't fault him for that. It was his job to protect the man who pays him. But somehow the direction of the conversation was taking a turn not originally intended. The talk was supposed to be about how to generate some money by selling the actual, physical lyrics to take care of, as Bob said:

"Your Ma!"

This situation was different. I was speaking with an attorney who appeared to be throwing up roadblocks to the sale of even one lyric. However, I had a secret weapon he hadn't counted on, and I had done my own bit of homework. We said our goodbyes having agreed to talk in the next day or so.

The next day I was watching the clock when the phone rang. It was the lawyer. His tone was different. About thirty seconds into the call, after we exchanged the normal pleasantries at the start of a phone conversation, he says right out of the blue:

"Just give me a number. How much will it take for Mr. Dylan to satisfy his obligation to you?"

That take on things had never crossed my mind. I don't know if those were Bob's words, or the way Mr. Q was used to lawyering.

"Oh, so that's the deal?" I answered. "OK, let's do the math. When Bob lived with us my parents left 50 cents out for him every morning so he could get around during the day and get something to eat to keep him going until he got home at night. That's $3.50 a week. Granted that was a long time ago, but let's make it all relative. At the most my parents were making $80 a week before taxes. That's the high-income estimate. They had very little money, if any, in the bank. Let's say that $3.50 represented about 4% of what they had at any given time. But to be conservative, cut it by half making it an even 2%. Bobs got to be worth $100 million. I'm happy for him. He earned it and deserved every penny. 2% of $100 million is $2 million. Have him make out a check to my mother for $2 million and we'll call it even."

There was dead silence on the other end of the phone. Hey, I didn't ask the question. He did. Anyway, he had no idea about the real key to the relationship. Before he broke the silence, I beat him to it.

"Let me set the record straight. Do you think my parents gave anything to Bob because they thought he was going to be rich and famous and get a big reward? They did it because they loved him like a son, and I loved him like a brother. When you love someone, you do it unconditionally with the hope they find their own direction in life and achieve their dreams no matter how big or small. The reward is the joy of seeing that they turned out okay. THAT'S the payoff. We are all very proud of him, how he used his potential and what he's accomplished with his life. Furthermore, regarding the lyrics, you're maneuvering to put us in a worse off position than had we not spoken with Bob at all. We didn't have to ask permission to sell the lyrics. We did it out of honor and respect. We already legally own them because he gave them to us 30 years ago. The proof of that is all on tape. Since Bob had no objection to the sale in the recent talk, I had with him there's really nothing more you can do for us. I know you must be a very busy man but thank you for your time."

With that I said "Goodbye!"

He never called again and a short time later some of the lyrics were sold.

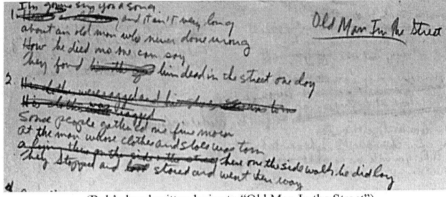

(Bob's handwritten lyrics to "Old Man In the Street")

As for it's all on tape....

CHAPTER 12:
THE RECORDER IS ON

Two years after his first paying gig at Gerde's and two days after his April 12, 1963, solo concert at Town Hall Bob dropped by our apartment. He hadn't had a chance to talk to my parents the day of his Town Hall performance even though they'd attended. This was the first chance he had to get free. It had been his most important engagement to date. Our tape recorder was on while he sat on the couch, me right next to him, and started to tune my guitar.

"This is a treat, Bobby, for me," my mother says.

He does a song called "James Alley Blues." Mom laughs.

"Is that a new one?"

"Nah," he says.

"Here's a couple of verses to one song. I never did get it done." He sings them.

"Something like that. I never did write it down," he says.

He starts fingerpicking another melody I'd never heard before.

"This was a guitar and harmonica sound."

It is an instrumental.

"Bobby, you're writing music now?" asks my mother.

"Oh no. I just used to play that with guitar and harmonica."

Dad offers to give him a harmonica as Mom says:

"Cousin Leslie sends her love."

A big grin appears on Bob's face.

"She's nice. I like her."

"She's special, Bobby, very special."

For a moment all is quiet. You can hear the far away street noises, the ticking of the living room clock. No sense of urgency. Peaceful. A total respite from the pace of the outside world.

Bob's voice breaks the silence.

"You've heard Hollis Brown, haven't you? You heard that? That's... I sang that at Town Hall. Hollis Brown."

"Yeah!" I blurt out a bit loud.

"That other one isn't on the record, is it?" my mother asks.

"What?"

"Hard Rain," she tells him.

"Oh, no... Here's one..."

He is about to play something else when my mother lets out a sigh:

"He won't do it. He said it's too long, too hard. He doesn't feel like singing it."

Bob starts to get fidgety.

"It's sort of... Here's one..."

My mother interjects:

"You mean I can't listen to it myself in the afternoon, playing it quietly? A piece of poetry like that I want to hear, Bobby."

His second album, 'The Freewheeling,' which contained the song, would not be out for another month and a half and Bob had not mentioned its impending release to my parents.

The atmosphere is palpable. A little scene within the scene has begun. He knows it. How effective will his footwork be?

"I'll do it for ya. I'll do it for ya. I don't feel... I... It's hard. It's hard to sing it."

"I know it's very hard. But it'll be another year before you come and do it. By that time, you'll be overseas, someplace," my mother sighs, either sorrowful or disappointed. There is a difference. I couldn't figure out which. She loved that song.

"Oh, here's one," he says, as if he found his long-lost wallet.

"My parents raised me tenderly I was their only son..."

Another one I hadn't heard before. It was funny, though. No, not the song, but the way he started it. His voice cracked. It was the wrong key. He stops and tries a different key... Wrong one, again. He moves the capo.

"Can't hardly find the right key," he exclaims.

He tries another. Not right. He fiddles around some more with the capo. It's not the great Bob Dylan putting on an act. It's just Bob at home trying to figure out the right note to begin.

Finally, he gets a key he is comfortable with.

"That's a good key," he announces and goes into the song.

It is a projection so natural, you believed it was a personal experience that really happened to him. He called it "Long Time Gone."

"Oh gee," says Mom. "Is that new? Is it yours?"

"Oh yeah, yeah."

"Sounds like it," she exclaims.

"It sounds like Bobby's. It's got his trademark on it," adds my father.

But, there is still the issue of "A Hard Rain's A-Gonne Fall." He is trying to delay doing it when he says:

"It's hard to sing it."

My mother sighs again.

"The most beautiful piece of poetry you won't do. Aaah...

"Want to hear a hobo song?" Bob hurriedly asks.

"Sure," says Dad.

Bob glances sideways at Mom.

It turns out the performance of "Only A Hobo" is even more humorous than what happened when he was trying to find the right key for "Long Time Gone." That's probably because he was still trying to figure out a way of not having to do "Hard Rain" and, at the same time, not disappoint Mom too badly. He really must have been working on that thought, because halfway through the song...

"Oh, wait. I forgot that one completely," he rattles.

There he is, strumming away, playing the same chord, no words, his eyes going up and down, side to side, trying to remember the rest of the song and still trying to come up with a way...

Then, suddenly...

"Uh... Ah...Want to hear, want to hear the rest of it?"

Without missing a beat, or waiting for an answer, he starts in mid-sentence exactly where he left off. He finishes the song, strums the last chord with a little flourish and turns to me:

"Pete, do you want to hear how I do 'House of The Rising Sun' now?"

He does an abbreviated version, using only one minor chord, up-tempo, but like a monotone dirge. I think he made the arrangement up on the spot. It was interesting. Having done it so differently, though, than before, reminded me of something.

"Remember 'See That My Grave Is Kept Clean' you did on your first album?" I ask.

"Yeah," he says.

"You used to do it differently."

"I did?"

"Yes. You played it with a different picking style."

"How?"

I explain it to him the best I can.

While we are trying to figure it out my mother walks over to the desk in the living room, opens one of the drawers, takes out some papers and says to Bob:

"'Talking Bear Mountain Blues' right here."

He looks up. The guitar playing stops.

"What? 'Talking...'"

"Mountain Blues," finishes my mother.

"Talking Mountain Blues," my father repeats.

"Oh, is that it?"

He is very surprised.

In her hands are pages of his handwritten lyrics she had so carefully saved and protected for him while he was living with us... plus a couple of books he had written in.

"There it is. Six o'clock in the morning he wrote it...," she muses. "You added a lot of different verses with it."

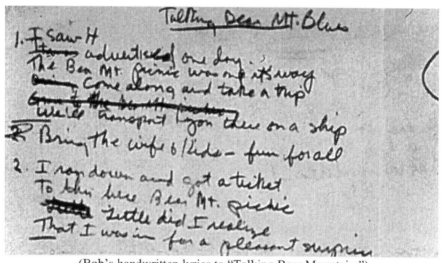

(Bob's handwritten lyrics to "Talking Bear Mountain.")

He starts leafing through them.

"I left out whole verses I never sing. There's a verse here. I just saw this."

He continues leafing through the rest of the papers.

"Well, it's your property if you want it," says my mother, laughing.

Bob stops for a moment and looks up.

"Nah, you can keep 'em."

He leaf's a little more.

"I hate to say it," as he says it, "could you bring that 'Sing Out' in here?"

"Sure," says Mom.

'Sing Out' was a current folk magazine that printed articles as well as song lyrics by old and new performers.

She goes to get it then hands it to him. He looks through it and retunes the guitar.

My mother takes the microphone...

"Let me bring it closer to your voice, Bobby, so it gets it."

He's just looked over the words to his song, "The Ballad Of Donald White." He starts to sing…

For those who are not familiar with that song, you can look up the words anywhere, or in his book "Writings and Drawings." It is based on a true story. The subject is a man who commits a murder and is executed. The song breaks new ground because it's the first time anybody wrote one dealing with the psychological effect societal actions, or lack of, can have on an individual psyche.

It questions who must share the blame for the murder which may have been preventable with proper environment, education etc.; an indictment of the inadequacy of the prison system and how people, when they are forgotten, pushed to the side, or ignored can lead to tragic consequences. It is a metaphoric, behavioral thesis expressed in music. A radical departure for word usage in the song medium.

Gil Turner, a contemporary of Bob's, the first one to sing "Blowing in the Wind" on stage right after Bob wrote it, said in a conversation with Bob and Pete Seeger:

"Well, I think "Donald White," is historic in the sense that it's the first psychological song of the modern generation I've heard."

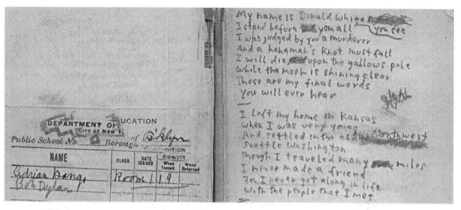

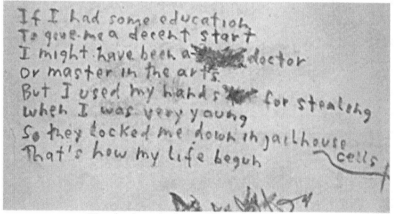

(Handwritten lyrics to "Donald White)
-From the William Pagel archives-

While Bob was living with us, my father talked to Bob about Clarence Darrow, the attorney who had defended Nathan Leopold and Richard Loeb in their 1924 sensational murder trial in Chicago. My father had great admiration and respect for Darrow for many reasons. He explained Darrow's lifelong contention that psychological, physical, and environmental influences — not a conscious choice between right and wrong — can determine human behavior. Regarding that specific case, he explained how Darrow used his riveting oratory skills with very forceful conviction in his summation arguing those points in an attempt to spare the two teenage boys from a death penalty. At the time, in a court setting, it was a unique and innovative approach to the determinants of an individual's action. In 1959 a movie based on the trial titled "Compulsion" with Orson Welles as Darrow was released. My father's telling the story made such an impression on me I went to see the movie as soon as I could.

There was another movie made in 1949 titled "Knock On Any Door" with Humphrey Bogart and John Derek. The script was on a similar topic of a young man from the slums played by John Derek who commits a murder and is defended by an attorney played by Humphrey Bogart. At the end the attorney makes an impassioned appeal to the judge for leniency based on the psychological, physical and environmental influences society may have had in shaping an individual's choice of behavior in any given circumstance. Is society partly responsible for the negligence in dealing with the well-being of the less fortunate, thus contributing to the actions of the young man? Knowing Bob's fascination with movies I've sometimes wondered if this movie, or the conversation with my father, could have contributed to the context for framing the plight of Donald White in a similar fashion in song. Where does the tipping point in the choice of approach come from? Where is the trigger? Whatever the reason, it is Bob who had the vision to forge a breakthrough of new expression in the music medium.

Bob finishes the rendition, which is still on the tape, that just grabs you and chills to the bone.

Another recorded version was later officially released by Folkways records using his alias, "Blind Boy Grunt." That rendition pales in comparison to this one. In fact, every rendition of every song he does on the various 28th St. tapes are far superior, more emotionally charged and powerful, than any of the different versions on the officially released recordings, or other versions that appear on any other tapes which have surfaced. That's not a biased opinion. Anyone familiar with Bob's work who has heard the original 28th St. master tapes, in a secure setting, has felt the same way. The fidelity of all the original tapes are studio quality and every nuance clear as a bell.

"Beautiful, beautiful," my father says.

"That's in 'Sing Out'," says Bob.

After a short pause Bob remarks out of nowhere:

"You know... you know who's fault I think it is? The Arabs."

"The Arabs?" questions my father.

"Yeah, for didn't they invent the zero?"

"That's true," Dad agrees.

The phone rings. My mother goes into her bedroom to answer it. It's my aunt. As soon as she leaves Bob says:

"Yeah... Okay, I'll sing you that one."

Only he knows why he decided to finally do "Hard Rain" right then. He'd done his best to put it off all evening. Maybe it was a twofer - for Eve and aunt Gig at the same time. Gig could certainly hear it through the phone. Maybe it was the look my father gave him as my mother was walking to the bedroom. It just clicked in his head it was now or never. He decided on now.

Two things about that performance are remarkable. Halfway through the opening line he starts trying some alternate words before shifting back to the original ones. The second was where he reached down inside to do that performance. He felt comfortable enough, as if he were almost completely isolated, no one critical, just peering into himself trying to figure out what he had written and where it had come from. There was no shield around him. Never or since have I, or my folks, heard him pull out every line like that. It was truly like an anguish from the gates of

Hell. When he said, "that's a hard song to sing," his definition of 'hard' is not in the dictionary. That rendition is six minutes of something words cannot adequately describe. The only adequate description is the performance itself.

My mother comes out of the bedroom and looks at him.

"Thank you, Bobby," she says with her most deep, heartfelt appreciation.

He is quiet for a moment as everything is osmosing. He looks over at my father.

"What time is it?"

"It's twenty after nine," says my father looking at his watch.

CHAPTER 13: OUT OF THE BOTTLE

June 1961 arrived. I was still trying to get home as fast as I could from school so I could catch Bob before he left on his nightly rounds. My guitar had nylon strings. What I really wanted was a steel string guitar like Bob's, or Jack Elliott's. Those were REAL guitars. I'd been fortunate before Bob started staying with us to get regular access to a steel string guitar thanks to Howard, downstairs.

In April, Howard got the Martin guitar advertising account as photographer. I would go downstairs and have my pick of any of several new Martin D-18's or D-28's to play. Howard took them home at night after photographing them at his studio. Their only drawback was the feel of a new steel string guitar is a bit stiff. Nothing beats the feel and sound of a broken in, well-travelled steel string guitar. As far as I was concerned Bob's 00-17 Martin was the best guitar in the entire world. Some nights when Bob went out, he'd leave his guitar behind. It would be sitting in its case underneath the five-foot-long coffee table in the living room. The coffee table was about a foot and a half wide and placed parallel to the couch he slept on. On those nights I would take it out and practice. I had asked him the first day he started staying with us if I could play it when he wasn't around.

"Sure, Pete. Anytime," he said.

In the late afternoon, one early June day, I came back from school after a detour to the grocery store. My mother and Bob were in the kitchen talking. I could see he was sitting forward in the rocking chair with his guitar in his hands. This time the sound coming out of it was unlike anything I was familiar with. If I'd heard that sound somewhere before I wasn't paying attention. But, this was Bob, and that sound immediately caught my ear. It wasn't the normal finger or flat-picking chording style. It was kind of this slinky, high, slithery noise. When I walked into the kitchen I saw, covering his left pinky finger, something that looked like the top of my mother's lipstick holder. In fact, it was the top of my mother's lipstick holder.

Earlier Bob had asked:

"Eve, do you have any lipstick in the house?"

"What, you have a new girlfriend you haven't told us about yet, Bobby?"

"Nah. I need the top of the lipstick case to put on my finger so I can get a certain sound out of the guitar. I found out about it from an old, black blues player while I was passing through the South."

Mom smiled at him:

"For you, of course. Let me go get it."

As she smiled, she was thinking:

"That young man has as likely been down South learning guitar tricks from an old, black blues guitar player as the moon is made of cheese."

She kept the thought to herself and came back into the kitchen with the top of the lipstick container and gave it to him.

"Is this what you are looking for?"

"Yep, Eve. It's just right."

"So, Bobby, what did your blues man friend teach you?"

She smiled at him, again.

He started to show her.

This is the point I came home carrying the groceries. I put the bags on the kitchen table, sat down on one of the stools, and started staring at Bob without saying a word.

"Hey, Pete, how are you doing today?"

"You have to teach me that," came right out of my mouth.

My mother rolled her eyes and looked at me:

"Aren't you forgetting something?"

"What?" I replied.

"Don't you think you better put the groceries away first?"

My mother looked at Bob. He looked at her. With an exasperated sigh I began unpacking the groceries and putting them in the refrigerator. As soon as I finished, I was right back on the stool.

"So, how do you do that, Bobby?"

Boy, I was being pushy. As usual, he had a ready response.

"Well, Pete, it's simple and it's not."

He knew that would fluster me for a moment. It was his good-natured way of letting me know my manners needed a little brushing up.

"Some people use a glass type rather than a metal one because they feel it slides over the strings easier," he explained.

"Oh," I said, not yet fully grasping what he was talking about.

"It's called bottleneck/slide guitar. It's good is because if you're just playing regular chords, or an open tuning, and throw in a slide it varies the overall sound and makes it more interesting."

Anyone who is familiar with the playing of Bonnie Raitt knows the kind of technique Bob was talking about. I got to meet her several years later when she asked Kevin to manage her, but his schedule couldn't accommodate it.

Bob continued:

"The secret is in the tuning of the strings. I have a few no one's used. When you slide your finger you can cover more than one string and put your other fingers down to get your chords."

It did sound a bit confusing. He lowered the pitch of one string, raised the pitch on another; made all sorts of combinations, but didn't show me all the variations right away. There were too many. That, combined with his fingerpicking... I had never heard anything like it and I wanted to learn it. From that day on, whether he was sitting in the living room or kitchen, if I walked in with a lipstick holder in my hand, he automatically knew what I wanted.

"Ok, Pete, I have just enough time to show you a couple of new slides and then you'll have to practice on your own. I won't always be here to show you."

A short time later he came home with his friend, Danny Kalb. He introduced him to my parents as the best blues guitar player around. I don't know what Bob had told him about us, but after a few minutes Danny starts talking to my father and asking him about Organized Labor. Out of the blue my dad asks him:

" Danny, is your father's name Fred?"

"Yes, but how did you know?"

"I saw pictures of you as a baby."

The look on Bob's face... the look on Danny's face...

It seems my father and Danny's father had been friends from way back when.

Bob turned the conversation back to music.

"What was that guitar run you played last night?

Bob almost sounded like me asking questions.

"Which one?" Danny asked.

"You know the one. It goes da, da, boom, chuck, bend, oomph."

He was speaking in a musical shorthand they both understood.

"Oh, yeah, I remember."

That was the kicker. Out comes Bob's guitar right into Danny's hands immediately followed by a harmonica into Bob's.

Bob was right. Danny could really play the blues like nobody's business. It was also one of the few times I ever heard Bob playing strictly straight up raw blues harmonica. It was a style completely different than when he played his guitar and harmonica at the same time; different than any of the times I heard him when he'd accompanied other people. It just got better and better.

In 1966 Danny, along with his friend, Al Kooper, formed the core of what you might call one of the first 'Supergroups,' "The Blues Project." Al had already worked with Bob, playing the iconic organ part on Bob's recording of "Like A Rolling Stone."

CHAPTER 14:
JUNE 17,1961 - ABOUT THE CALIFORNIA BROWN EYED GIRL

Having finished my final exams, I now had all the time in the world to spend with Bob when he was around. Things were on an even keel for a few days when he came home, once again, all excited. It was on a Saturday because my aunt Gig was visiting. Saturday was her normal visiting day. She and Bob got along very well. They liked discussing poetry with each other, dropping obscure names of people I never heard of... and I was familiar with a lot of poets. Our floor to ceiling bookcases were crowded with every type of literature imaginable. My father was the real reader in the family. I think he'd read every book in every library there ever was. I know that's impossible, but it felt that way. Bob looked, at that point, like he was going to be a close second. He was going through each bookshelf two books at a time. As Bob came through the front door his words came tumbling out:

"Got to call Avril. Eve, get the phone.”

He was almost out of breath.

"Hold your horses. What's going on?” she asked.

"Wrote a song for her. Got to call her collect and sing it to her.

"Bobby, we know it's important to you, but you can't call Avril collect."

"Why not?”

"Avril doesn't have any money. She can't afford a collect call.”

"Avril doesn't have any money. She can't afford a collect call." For a second, he looked like a door had been slammed in his face and he couldn't think fast enough to avoid the impact. It was a quandary. He didn't want to burden my parents with the cost of the call, but he had forgotten, for the moment, Avril had no money either.

"Bobby, don't worry," she says. "I think we can swing it. We'll call her for you, directly."

She gets out her address book to look up Avril's number. Bob hurries to get his guitar out from under the tea table. He straps it over his shoulder. My mother carefully dials the number. One, two, three rings.

"Hello?" says a voice on the other end of the line.

Bob is fidgety, like a boy on his first date after he rings the doorbell knowing the girl's parents will answer it.

"Avril?" says Mom.

"No", Avril's not here. Who's calling?"

"This is Eve McKenzie. Avril stayed with us when she was in New York."

"I'm her mother," replies the voice. "My daughter told us about your family. Thank you so much for looking after her."

"Oh, no need to thank us. It was our pleasure. She was a joy to have around."

She cups the phone and mouths the words:

"Avril's not there."

For the second time in less than a few heartbeats one glance at Bob and he looks like a door hit him in the face again.

"Mrs. Weber, no cause for any kind of alarm," my mother responds, "but I promised Avril before she left, I would call her and I've been lax. Do you know when she will be back?"

"I don't know. She's visiting friends."

Poor Bob. He couldn't sit down, was rocking the guitar from side to side, eyes like exasperated lasers on Mom, as if trying to will something through the phone line

"Mrs. Weber, I don't mean to impose, but do you know the friends she is visiting?"

Bob's shoulders are raised.

"Yes, I do, Mrs. McKenzie."

"Call me Eve. You wouldn't happen"...

..."to have the number?" Mrs. Weber finishes the sentence.

"Yes," says my mother.

"As a matter of fact, I do. Would you like it?"

"It would be most appreciated."

She writes down the phone number and looks over at Bob with a smile. He knows exactly what her smile means and is now standing up straight, shoulders down.

"Thank you so much, Mrs. Weber. You really do have a wonderful daughter."

She hangs up the phone.

"Well?" asks Bob.

"I have to make another phone call and we'll see."

Bob's shoulders are slightly raised again.

Mom dials. We all hear the rings on the other end.

"Hello?"

It was a man.

"Hello," says my mother. "Is Avril Weber there?"

"Who's calling?"

"My name is Eve McKenzie."

"Hold on a second, I'll see."

My mother could hear different voices in the background.

"Avril, there's an Eve McKenzie on the phone."

One, two...

"Eve?"

"Yes, Avril."

"Oh, Eve, how are you? I'm so glad you called."

"I'm fine, Avril. I hope everything is working out for you. I just spoke with your mother, and she gave me this number."

"Yes, I'm at a friend's house. My brother is also here."

"That's nice. It seems you're in good company."

My mother continues:

"One of the reasons I called is because there's someone here who would like to say 'hello.' I'll put him on."

Mom hands the phone to Bob who looks at this point... well, he just looks.

"Hey, Avril," he says.

"Bobby?"

"Yep. And I have something for ya. Hold on a minute."

He hands the phone back to my mother. She holds it up near his mouth.

"I wrote this for ya."

The next part I didn't learn until I recently when I spoke to Avril's brother, Eric. Eric is a professional photographer who lives out west in the Sierra Nevada region.

As soon as Avril heard it was Bob on the phone and he had written something for her she motioned her brother and his friend to crowd around and get their ears as close to the receiver as possible. The set up now is Avril's small group huddled around the phone in San Francisco and at 28th St. my mother holding up the receiver with my dad, aunt and me also gathered around. Bob positions himself so he can get the best balance between his voice and guitar to sing into that single, long distance microphone. He clears his throat and goes right into his number he called "My California Brown Eyed Baby."

It is a very emotional moment. Laughter, sniffling, clapping...

When he finished Mom handed him the phone so he could take it into my parent's bedroom and have some privacy.

I believe "California Brown Eyed Baby" is the first original song Bob wrote in NYC mentioned in print. It appears in the program notes of his first solo concert at Carnegie Chapter Hall on Saturday, November 4, 1961.

> "I started writing my own songs about four or five years ago. First song was to Brigit Bardot, for piano. Thought if I wrote the song I'd sing it to her one day. Never met her. I've written hillbilly songs that Cal Perkins from Nashville, Tenn. sings. I write Talking Blues on Topical things. "California Brown Eyed Baby" has caught on. Noel Stookey gave me the idea for the "Bear Mountain Song" I wrote it overnight but I wasn't there. Never sing it the same way twice because I never wrote it down.

(Bob did write down the lyrics to "Talking Bear Mountain."
See image in Chapter 12)

When he sang that song, it was the first time we were aware Bob had started writing more original material. Other than "Song to Woody" the rest of his repertoire had been traditional, or else arranged by him with some word changes.

There are no recordings, as far as I know, of Bob singing the song, but I never forgot the melody. It was set to the tune of the old standard, "Columbus Stockade." The only recording of it is with the radio station, WBAI, in New York City on a "Bob" 50th birthday night. It's me trying my best to do it justice.

written by Bob Dylan
Summer 1981

The rain is fallin' at my window
My thoughts are sad forevermore
I'm thinkin' about my brown eyed darlin'
The only one that I adore

She's my California brown eyed baby
The only one I think about today
She's my California brown eyed baby
Livin' down San Francisco way

Sadly I look out of my window
Where I can hear the raindrops fall
My heart is many thousand miles away
Where I can hear my true love call

Now boys don't you start to ramble
Stay right there in your home town
Find you a gal that really loves you
Stay right there and settle down

(Bob's handwritten lyrics to "California Brown Eyed Baby."
My Mother's handwriting is at the top}

CHAPTER 15: JUNE 18, 1961

The morning after the San Francisco call I woke up late. Bob was already having his breakfast. It was Sunday.

"Morning, Pete."

"You're up early," I said.

"You're up late," he said back.

I sat down at the kitchen table. Yesterday's experience reminded me that Bob had hightailed it out of town shortly after he finished his first paying gig at Gerde's a couple of months earlier.

"What happened to you right after Gerde's?"

"Well, I went to an event called "The Indian Neck Festival" in Connecticut. I met a lot of new people and hung out with Mark Spoelstra. He plays 12 string guitar."

We met Mark later on. He was the nicest person you could hope to meet. He was a Quaker, and my folks became very fond of him. I recently found a tape he recorded with Bob one night when they were visiting. Kevin had introduced them.

Around 1 pm Kevin came by and suggested we all go down to Washington Square.

"I've got a couple other things I've got to do today. Why don't you and Pete go down," Bob says to Kevin.

"All right. By the way, are you using your guitar this afternoon?" Kevin asks.

"Wasn't planning on it."

"Good. Then we can take it with us when we go to the park."

It was more a statement than a question.

"We'll be back in a couple of hours," he says.

We are off, Bob's guitar in hand. When we arrive the usual size crowds and the regular groups are there. Kevin looks around for a spot that is far enough away from the other performers so you can hear an individual sing. He finds one about 30 feet northwest of the central fountain. He takes out the guitar and hands it to me.

"What are you doing, Kevin?" I ask.

"I'm giving you the guitar so you can sing. Make sure it's in tune."

"But, I thought we came down here so you could perform? I don't think …"

He cuts me off.

"No, Pete. We came down here so you could. You're as good as a lot of the other people here. It's time to give it a try."

This I hadn't been prepared for, sometimes being a bit on the shy side performing in front of a group of people without notice.

While my stomach was in my throat, I didn't want to look like a wuss in front of him. The only way out of it was to play and get it over with. I begin to play...

Nothing happens. No crowd starts to gather. I see Kevin looking at me and hear his voice:

"You know, Pete, if you were in college you'd get an A in whispering."

He takes the guitar from me and straps it on himself.

"Watch and learn."

He begins to strum. I couldn't believe the volume of his voice. Loud would be an understatement as he belts out one song and then starts another. Lo and behold, there's suddenly a small, but growing crowd gathering around listening. He looks at me.

"Your turn."

Then he announces:

"I am glad you are all enjoying yourselves. I am now turning over the festivities to my friend here. He's very good and is going to sing a couple of songs."

I wanted to choke him, but he was too tall. The guitar is strapped around my shoulder. There are now a whole bunch of strangers staring at me with expectations. I start to sing...

I don't remember much about the performance. I do know I felt a bit protected because I had Bob's guitar in front of me. A detail I clearly recall is hearing someone uttering something that didn't sit right with me.

"Yeah, for your information, this is a professional guitar I'm playing," I snapped back.

I know that must sound ridiculous, but no one was going to say anything rude which included something that belonged to Bob. When I finished, we packed up.

"Hey, for your first time out here, kid, not bad," said Kevin.

We arrived home. Bob was still there. Wait a minute... I thought he said he had things to do.

"The kid did all right. Thanks for the guitar, Bob."

Bob nodded and it hit me. It was all planned out beforehand - Kevin just happening to show up, the ease which he commandeered Bob's guitar, Bob still here when we got back as if he were waiting for a report. My parents were smiling. It was a conspiracy. While it wasn't something I could fully grasp at the time, I realized later it was a coordinated effort by Bob, my parents and Kevin to help me get over my public shyness and build my confidence.

CHAPTER 16:
SHUFFLE THE DECK AND PAPERS

It now appeared Bob had been bitten by the writing bug, but that just added to his bag of surprises. That bag also included several card tricks. He was very proud of his abilities with the deck and found in me the perfect audience, or perhaps the perfect guinea pig. I constantly tried to pry his secrets out of him, but Bob always answered:

"You'll eventually figure it out, Pete."

I don't remember the tricks as being that intricate, but he sure made them look easy. Then again, you probably didn't have to be that skilled to dazzle a 15-year-old. He had a favorite. The first time he did it, we were sitting together at the kitchen table soon after his singing, telephone rendition to Avril.

"You want to see a special trick?"

I immediately said "yes," and went over to one of the kitchen drawers and took out a deck of cards. They weren't marked in any way; just a regular deck, which I brought back to the table. Bob shuffled them a few times then handed them back to me.

"Shuffle them some more," he said.

I did as he requested and gave the cards back to him.

"Now watch carefully."

He went through the deck, looking at each card, face up, all 52 of them. It took a little over a minute. Then he placed the entire deck face down, looked me in the eye and said, very seriously:

"Are you ready?"

Of course I was ready. Why was he drawing it out? As soon as I asked myself the question I realized it was Bob doing a performance. He was drawing it out to maximize the drama. He looked down at the cards and tapped the top one.

"King of spades," he announced. He turned it over and it was, indeed, the king of spades.

"10 of Hearts," he said, after tapping the second card. Again, he had it right.

"3 of Clubs."

He turned the third card over and it was the 3 of Clubs. He went through the next 20 cards the same way, getting each one correct. I remember him checking the expression on my face each time he turned a card over. I'm sure my eyes were getting bigger, and my jaw dropped a little more each time he turned one face up. He was having a fine old time judging from the look on his face. Finally, I couldn't stand it anymore.

"How do you do that?" I exclaimed.

I was insisting, more than asking.

"But, Pete, the effect would be ruined if I told you."

He studied my puzzled face, seeing my wheels spinning, trying to solve the mystery. He burst out laughing and almost fell off his stool. He couldn't contain himself. And at my expense. I wanted to shake it out of him, but he was having too good a time.

He never did tell me how he did it, but much later, I figured it out. It hadn't been a trick at all. In that short time when he flipped through the cards - a little over a minute - he had memorized the entire deck.

That night, about three o'clock in the morning, I woke up to what I thought was the sound of a guitar being played in the kitchen. I was only half awake, but it sounded nice. I fell right back to sleep.

The next morning, after my father had gone to work, Bob and I sat down to the breakfast my mother had made and I noticed a couple of pages of handwritten words next to Bob's plate.

"Hey," Bob announced, "wrote part of a song last night. I was using your guitar, Pete. Wanna hear it?"

"Yes," my mother and I said, simultaneously.

This was the first time Bob openly shared what was on those sheets of paper on the kitchen table. He sang a couple of verses glancing down at one of the sheets. It was something about swinging onto an old subway car holding a guitar.

"Not finished yet, but you get the idea. You like it?" he asked.

Heck, I thought it was Shakespeare.

"It's excellent. You've got a nice way with words," Mom responded.

"Yeah. I wrote it last night when I got back and was sitting in the kitchen."

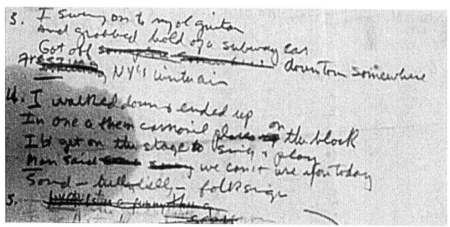

(Bob's handwritten lyrics to "Talking New York")

Now I knew for certain what had half awakened me the night before. When you think about it, it was thoughtful of Bob to use my guitar instead of his. Mine had nylon strings and was much quieter, so he wouldn't disturb me.

Never a procrastinator, my mother said:

"You want me to put them in the drawer with your other papers, so they won't get lost?"

"Yeah. Already memorized the words. If I need them, I'll know where to look."

That would become the routine when he wrote at night. He would come home at a late hour, sit at the kitchen table with my guitar, or sometimes without it. When he was ready, he'd say:

"Wrote something. Wanna hear it?"

It didn't matter where he left the scraps of paper. Whether it was the kitchen table, or the table next to the couch, when it was cleanup time, into the drawer all the papers went. We didn't always know if it was another original song. We only knew that he'd share it when he was ready. My parents never pressured him about it. I was a little more forward. I didn't ask every day, but I did take liberties on several occasions.

"You write anything new, Bobby?" I would ask.

Almost always, I got the same response.

"Pete, you'll be the first to know."

It made me feel special, like it was our shared secret, like newspaper reporter getting a big scoop. But, as curious as I was, I never read the pieces of paper left on the table if I got up first. Nor did I peek in the drawer when Bob was out to see what he was writing. It was difficult to restrain myself from doing so because of my youthful inquisitiveness, but those writings were private... the drawer was off limits. He didn't always make me wait, though. Sometimes he'd just push a piece of paper over to me when we were both at the table and say:

"You can look at it, if you want, Pete."

We eventually heard all the songs. A lot of people describe them as mostly derivative—they follow certain talking blues patterns of Woody Guthrie and others, or have very basic, or even borrowed melodies—but there was nothing derivative about the words he strung together. When we heard him do the finished "Talking New York" (the song with the line about swinging onto an old subway car) we knew it was special.

Remember, you have to view things within the context of the times they arose. That song just jumped right out at you: not a forced phrase; a seamless flow from beginning to end, and it was funny. Those works, even in that familiar vein, were original and different. "Talking New York" was one of his two original compositions on his first album. The other was "Song to Woody." I'm not a literary critic, but I believe I can recognize when something is exceptional. Take "Talking Bear Mountain Picnic Massacre Blues." When it begins it might sound like any number of other songs, but very quickly, you realize that it could only have been written by Bob Dylan. The style of humor and the use of the almost throw away phrase are so individualistic it might be the equivalent of a virtual fingerprint.

Bob instinctively grasped that the sensory part of songwriting as well as the intellectual; the way lyrics fall upon the ear are as important as how they engage the mind. His song, "Old Man In The Street," might not have the world's greatest storyline, but the sound of the language is what makes it memorable. He chose words specifically for the beginning consonant sounds, so when those words are strung together, they become jolting phonetically. The sound punches you, and the listening experience transcends the storyline. The song, which is about a specific event, becomes something bigger than its subject matter. Bob wasn't the only songwriter working this way; he just did it better, right out of the starting gate.

There is an irony, however, about some of Bob's writing that even he didn't know until years later. That's ironic in and of itself since Bob's body of work displays a deep understanding and mastery of its use. A conversation occurred between us years after he had moved out of our apartment that is its quintessential definition.

On his second album, "The Freewheelin' Bob Dylan," his song, "Bob Dylan's Blues," starts off with the spoken introduction:

"Unlike most of the songs written nowadays are being written uptown in Tin Pan Alley. That's where most of the folk songs come from nowadays. This... this wasn't written up there. This was written somewhere down in the United States."

About 100 feet to the west of the door to our building between Broadway and Fifth Avenue is a bronze plaque embedded in the sidewalk that has been there since before I was born. As a kid I'd explored every nook and cranny of that block along with little Dorcas and Sharon Neal from upstairs and the two children from the Chinese laundry across the street, Lee and his sister, Kim. We knew every inch of the place, so naturally, one of us discovered the plaque. I didn't think about it again until years later, long after Bob had made his mark. It was little Dorcas, now grown up still living upstairs, who brought it up in a conversation we were having about our childhood. Neither of us remembered exactly what it said so I told her I'd check it out. I did and kept the information in my back pocket.

At a certain point in my 1991 conversation with Bob I decided to mention the plaque, not yet telling him what I found on it.

As curious as Bob usually is, his first comment was:

"Plaques. People want to give me plaques all the time."

"Yes, Bob," I said, "but it is a very special plaque."

This was one of those rare times I knew I had an opening to tease him, so I drew it out a little. For once I knew something he didn't. I reminded him of his spoken introduction to "Bob Dylan's Blues." Then I told him about the inscription on the plaque. He was silent for a second, then only, "Hmmm."

In 1965, the documentary filmmaker, D.A. Pennebaker, shot a film called "Don't Look Back," chronicling Bob touring England. One scene shows Bob visiting Denmark Street, which was considered the Tin Pan Alley of London. A lot of famous English artists recorded there in the 1960s, having gravitated to it in the previous decade. I think Bob's curiosity had to do with the mystique—the history and lore filling the many music stores and guitar shops—and he probably wanted to soak up some of the ambience.

Tin Pan Alley was the nickname for a neighborhood in New York City where many of the songwriters and music publishing houses were all bunched together in the early part of the 20th century. It was the birthplace of 20th century American music. Works by George Gershwin, Irving Berlin, Cole Porter and many more first came out of there. It got the moniker "Tin Pan Alley" because of the cacophonous sounds of all the pianos banging away that filled the air. Bob had always pooh-poohed the American Tin Pan Alley as the birthplace of "I love you, you love me, icky dickey dickey dee." In fact, sometime in the late 1960's it is said he made a statement to the effect that he had single-handedly killed Tin Pan

Alley. In many photos of Tin Pan Alley, a sign reading "M.Witmark & Sons" adorns one building. It is also Bob's early publishing house and in 2010 Columbia released a record of Bob's compositions called "The Witmark Demos." The original M.Witmark & Sons' offices were on W. 28th St., just a stone's throw from 10 West before relocating uptown in the late teens, or early 1920s. They were just down the street from Leo Feist, one of the biggest sheet music publishers in the world. In the 1920s, the U.S. Government sued him and six other companies, including M.Witmark & Sons, under the Federal Antitrust Act.

Being the master of irony, Bob's "Hmmm" spoke volumes. He'd gotten it in a heartbeat.

"So, Bob," I laughed, "that means you're the greatest songwriter Tin Pan Alley ever produced."

I don't know in his comings and goings in and out of New York City if he ever took the time to go look at the plaque, but it reads:

A LANDMARK OF AMERICAN MUSIC
TIN PAN ALLEY
28th STREET BETWEEN FIFTH AND SIXTH
AVENUES WAS THE LEGENDARY TIN PAN ALLEY
WHERE THE BUSINESS OF THE AMERICAN
POPULAR SONG FLOURISHED DURING THE FIRST
DECADES OF THE TWENTIETH CENTURY.

(28th St. just west of Broadway)

(Bob in London where he visited Denmark Street 1965)

(My mother in 1991, 3 years before she died,
holding my nylon string guitar Bob used in
the kitchen to write songs late at night)

CHAPTER 17:
THE WRESTLER ARRIVES

"I'm going up to Cambridge, Massachusetts for a few days. Haven't been there before and I hear it's a happening scene," Bob said one morning out of nowhere.

When he saw the disappointment on my face, he had the perfect follow up. He knew about my Harvard dream.

"Pete, while I'm in Cambridge I'll have some free time. I hear one of the places I'm going to visit, Club 47, is only a couple of blocks from Harvard Square I'll do some campus scouting for you. When I get back, I can give you a first-hand report what it's like."

Pretty slick logic. Now he wasn't going just to meet other people, but to also check out Harvard for me. I even started getting enthusiastic about it and couldn't wait for him to get going. The sooner he went the sooner he'd be back and tell me how things were there.

Just as he was about to leave my father got a call from an old friend from his union days, Duke Livingston. Dad invited Duke and his wife, Millie, over. They arrived. After the intros Bob was out the door and on his way.

Duke Livingston was a bit younger than my dad. He was heavyset, but solid as a rock and had looked up to my father as one of the leaders of the National Maritime Union, acting as his bodyguard a few times back then. Like my father, he believed in the power of the pen and the dynamism of speech. I found out he had also been a professional wrestler. He showed me a few holds.

Bob later became fascinated when Duke would tell his wrestling stories.

(Duke and Millie Livingston)

Duke's wrestling tales were something else. It was all Show Biz. Not that Duke wasn't a genuine wrestler, because he could wrestle all right. If wrestling wasn't fixed, he'd still do well in the ring. Bob and I were both glued when he would later hold court explaining how it was staged and all the types of Damon Runyon-like characters attending the fights and inhabiting that world. Though some tales seemed tall, they were all true.

On any specific night Duke would meet beforehand with whomever he was to go up against. They would work out a series of choreographed moves to whip the crowd into a frenzy before the final takedown. Certain guys had worked with each other enough, so their inter-antics became second nature. All that remained was who would be the predetermined winner. He would laugh when describing having his opponent in a headlock, or vice versa; how they would talk to each other about their wives. Where they might go for a drink afterwards. Sometimes, they would tell each other jokes. They weren't supposed to laugh in the middle of the titanic struggle and would have to bite their lips trying to make the fiercest faces. It was the best acting job he ever had, and he could never understand how most of the crowd didn't get the whole business was phony. Bob loved hearing the stories. The more he heard the more details he wanted to know. When Duke was about to wrap it up Bob would say:

"Aw, c'mon, Duke, just one more."

"Ok, kid. For you one last one," he would answer.

The first night Duke came over I learned some more pieces of my Dad's background. Yet, as fascinating as that was for me, I already missed Bob. It was great to learn more about my dad's background, but he'd always be around I thought. Plenty of time. Bob, as much as I wanted it, I knew wouldn't. At least not in the same way. Then, after a short time, Bob was back with an enthusiastic attitude. I wanted to know every detail. Dad and Mom immediately came to his rescue.

"Pete, at least let Bobby sit down and catch his breath."

He sat down and my mother brought him a big glass of juice.

"So, how'd it go?" my father asks.

The first thing Bob says is:

"Pete, the Harvard campus and surroundings are beautiful. The architecture is great. You're really going to like it, particularly Harvard Square. You'll have a fine time there."

He'd kept his word and hadn't forgotten about me. Then he animatedly began telling us about some people he met he thought were cool. There was Richard Farina, a writer, musician, singer and Richard's then wife, Carolyn Hester. He played some guitar and harmonica with them. He liked the fact that Carolyn Hester, who was from Texas, had already recorded a couple of albums. He enjoyed his discussions with Dick Farina.

"He's an intellectual and a good writer."

Later, before Richard Farina died, he and Carolyn got divorced and Richard married Mimi Baez, Joan Baez's sister.

He told us about a guitar player named Eric Von Schmidt. He made a big impression on Bob. Not only did he have an enormous amount of song material Bob never heard before, but was also a superb visual artist.

"Pete, when you get to Cambridge you have to meet him."

Mr. Von Schmidt was an early influence on Bob. He taught him "Baby Let Me Follow You Down" and Bob put it on his first album. He gives full credit to Mr. Von Schmidt in a preamble to the song for teaching it to him.

I never did get to meet Mr. Von Schmidt in Cambridge, but I did get to meet Richard and Mimi Farina... all because of Suze Rotolo.

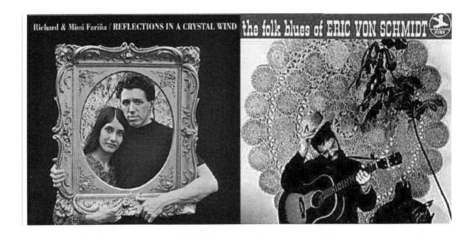

CHAPTER 18:

4/12/63 + 18 MONTHS TO RICHARD & MIMI

On October 24, 1964, Bob was going to play Symphony Hall in Boston. It was my sophomore year at college. I immediately got two tickets. A week before the concert I was walking down Mount Auburn Street in Cambridge right near campus and who do I run right into?... Suze Rotolo. She had been Bob's sweetheart since late July 1961. They'd had a storied romance for well over two years until the split came. She later wrote a book about the period called "A Freewheeling Time." You should read it.

She looked positively beautiful. I hadn't seen her since Bob's Town Hall concert seventeen months earlier. At the Town Hall concert on April 12, 1963, I was sitting in the first balcony with friends. Perfect view. My parents were in the orchestra section below. Bob was going through his repertoire wowing the crowd.

It was a big deal. This was Town Hall, New York City, a theater venue with a storied history. A solo concert there was considered a major step forward. Bob finished one song to terrific applause and then had to take a minute or so to change his harmonica. The Hall was quiet. Suddenly, out of nowhere, comes this loud voice from the audience.

"Do 'Riding Number Nine'."

For a split-second Bob stops on stage, then resumes putting in his new harmonica and turns back to the microphone. He gets into his stance, ready to go. Again, from amidst the crowd:

"Do 'Riding Number Nine'."

Again, he stops for a second. He puts his hand above his brow as if he is trying to see something. Then he takes his hand and points it up to somewhere in the audience.

"Shine a light up there," he says smiling.

He brings his hand back down, strums a chord and starts singing... It was not 'Riding Number Nine'.

After his last scheduled song, for an encore, he stood at the microphone holding several pieces of paper which he said was a poem he had written called "Last Thoughts On Woody Guthrie," and proceeded to recite it. I don't think he's ever done anything like that since, but it was a powerhouse... as good as any Harvard paper I ever read. Each line... bam, bam, bam. You could hardly hear anyone breathe; the audience was so quiet. He was in his own zip code, and everyone could feel it. What an ending. You had to be there...the thunderous applause.

I had to go to back and see him. When he'd done "A Hard Rain's A-Gonna Fall" the audience's collective jaw dropped. He sure learned how to give a history lesson when he sang "With God on Our Side."

I hopped up on the stage. That was the way to go to get to the dressing room. The first person I run into is Suze.

"Peter, was that you shouting out 'Riding Number Nine'?"

"Yes, it was," I replied.

She was almost laughing.

I squeezed backstage. Bob seemed in a fine mood.

"Hi, Pete. Like the show?"

It was obvious he and Suze had already talked about the 'shout out' from the crowd because the next thing he said was:

"That was you."

"Yeah," I answered, "but why didn't they shine a light when you pointed?"

He chuckled.

"Bobby, that Woody Guthrie poem was something else."

"You liked it?"

"Like it would be an understatement," I replied, and then told him I'd know in a few days which colleges had accepted me.

"Don't worry," he reassured me as he looked around the room.

"Where are your Mom and Dad? Didn't they come back with you?" he asked.

"They thought you would be inundated."

There were a lot of people backstage and this night being so important I figured I'd leave him alone saying "Good night," or something like that.

As I exited backstage Suze was waiting.

"Where are you going, Pete? There's a party happening in a little while. Why don't you bring anyone else you want who's here from your school? Here's the address. Get your friends together and come on over."

"Thanks, Suze. See you in a bit."

I immediately rushed back out front to try and corral as many classmates as I could. Off we went to a building on the upper West Side. It turned out to be the apartment of Peter Yarrow's mother (the Peter of Peter, Paul and Mary).

Bob and Suze were already there, as well as a bunch of other people seated in the living room. It was a bit noisy. I went over and whispered in Bob's ear. He nodded and I walked out of the living room with his Gibson J-50 guitar in hand and headed for the kitchen. My friends followed. We thought we'd have a little party on the side by ourselves.

Who should be sitting on one of the kitchen counters when we entered, but Ian Tyson of Ian and Sylvia. I immediately told him how much I liked his and Sylvia's music.

"Thank you. Oh, you've got Bob's guitar. You can play, right?

I flashed back to the first night Jack Elliott walked through Howard's door at 28th Street, over two years earlier, looking for Anne-Marie. How cocky I'd acted then before Jack Elliott diplomatically put me in my place.

"Well, you going to play that guitar or just admire its workmanship?" he continues.

"What? You'd like to hear a song?"

"I wouldn't ask if I didn't."

This time I was going to be cautious and measure my words.

"I haven't been playing that long."

"That doesn't matter. Everyone has to start somewhere."

"Don't be modest," one of the girls says and nudges me.

"He's really good," says another.

"Just great," I'm thinking. "Now there are expectations."

"Okay," I say, resigned. "Would you like to hear a song Bob does that you might not have heard?"

"By all means," as he leans back.

I decided to do "Riding Number Nine," the request I'd shouted out at the concert. When I finished he clapped a couple of times.

"That was nice."

"Thank you," I replied.

Before he had a chance to say, "Do you have another one?" I decided to quit while I was ahead.

"It was a real pleasure to meet you, Mr. Tyson. You have some new fans," referring to the girls with me.

"Thank you, young man."

I'm not sure all the girls wanted to leave the kitchen. He was very handsome. I went back into the living room to put Bob's guitar in its case. The talk was getting more boisterous.

"That was you I heard singing in the other room, Pete," Bob said more than asks.

"Yeah. I sang a song for Ian."

"Oh, Ian. Yeah, Ian's a good guy. I like him a lot."

"Well, it's getting late, and you know Mom," I told him.

He saw my friends watching from the living room entrance.

"Are those your school friends?" he asked.

"Yeah."

He nodded his head saying just loud enough for them to hear:

"Nice seeing all of you."

One of the girls waved back…

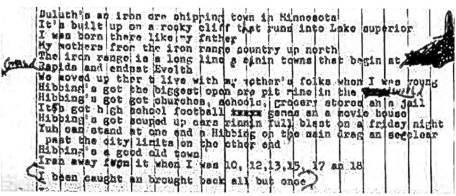

(Bob's typed "My Life In A Stolen Moment" with handwritten corrections.)

Eleven months later, in March 1964, even though half my college classmates had no idea who Bob Dylan was, I was excited when I saw the announcement he had been picked to perform for our "Freshman Jubilee Weekend" at Harvard on April 17, 1964. I immediately invited Ellie, who had been my girlfriend senior year in high school, to come along. I had introduced her to Bob one night in 1963 when he visited our apartment, and she was there.

Bob Dylan Concert

APRIL 17 at 8:15   RINDGE TECH

TICKETS at the COOP and at the door
-From the William Pagel archives-

We were sitting front row just left of center stage. The hall was full. At 8:15 sharp out came Bob with his signature entrance at the time - strumming his guitar while playing the harmonica as he walked to the microphone and without a word launched into "The Times They Are A Changin'." The whole place erupted with applause and whistles. A few songs later Joan Baez stepped out on stage and the place went double crazy.

It is hard to describe the chemistry and power those two had together at that time in music history. The connection between them, as well with the audience, was so intense if the Beatles had walked in at that moment the crowd might have said:

"Hi, boys, have a seat and watch the show."

No disrespect toward the Beatles. It's just that those two were so astonishing together, so perfectly in tune with each other, there was simply no room for anyone else on the stage.

The concert ended to a tremendous ovation. Lots of my friends, even some who hadn't heard of Bob before, tried to get backstage, pushing and jostling. Unfortunately for everyone, there were two enormous guards standing behind the rope at the entrance of the hallway that led backstage. They were not letting ANYONE through.

Well, there was no way I was NOT going to get to see Bob. After managing to get to the front of the line, Ellie next to me, I said to one of the guards:

"Could you please tell Mr. Dylan that Peter McKenzie is here."

"Yeah kid, lots of people want to meet Mr. Dylan," he curtly answered.

At least I had gotten his attention.

"If Mr. Dylan hears that I was here and was stopped from seeing him he is not going to be happy," I shot back.

There wasn't much else I could do at that point. I sounded like a smart ass mouthing off. Luckily, the other guard either sensed something, or figured I was full of it and was going to embarrass me in front of my friends. He turns to the first guard and with a slight smirk on his face says:

"I got it under control. Why don't you go back and tell Mr. Dylan this kid wants to see him. What's your name again?"

"Peter McKenzie."

"Ok," he says.

The guard walks slowly back to the dressing room. He leans inside the doorway and says something to somebody. After a slight pause he pivots and starts to hurry back down the corridor.

"Peter McKenzie? Is Peter McKenzie here?"

He had already forgotten my face; not that I blame him. He's seen thousands of faces like mine.

"Mr. Dylan wants to see him, immediately."

"That's me," I pipe up.

"Right this way," he says, unhooking the rope.

A whole throng surges trying to go in with me. The guards stop them all.

I look at Ellie.

"She's with me," I insist.

"He only wants to see you," says the guard, as he closes the rope behind me.

I look again at Ellie.

"I'll be waiting outside for you when you get back," she says.

I had temporary mixed emotions as I walked down the hallway because Ellie was still behind the rope. When I got to the dressing room door and poked my head inside I heard that voice...

"Pete, my Harvard man, how are you?"

It was Bob in the process of pulling up a change of pants. He was finished by the time I reached him and gave him a big hug.

"You know you're always great in my book," I said. "You had 'em all in the palm of your hand."

He smiled.

"I knew you'd be here tonight."

"How'd you know?" I asked.

"I just did," he smiled again.

"When I saw you were going to play here I told everyone I knew they had to hear you. The place was packed."

He smiled a third time.

"You should have seen the number of people trying to push through the rope to get backstage to meet you. The guards were so strict they wouldn't even let my girlfriend back with me."

"What's her name? I'll send word to let her through," he said.

"It's Ellie. I introduced you to her when you dropped by the apartment last year."

He thought for a moment.

"Oh yeah, I remember her. She was smart and pretty. Let's get her back here."

"That would be great," I answered. "She would've liked that, but she's already gone outside with everyone else and we're planning to see each other later. You know, there's a story about Ellie I never told."

"What's that?" he asked.

I could see by his eyebrows he was interested.

"About a year ago Ellie called me at the apartment all excited. 'Pete,' she said, 'why didn't you tell me you had a record out. I just heard it on the radio.'

"What do you mean," I replied.

"I just heard the end of it. I think it's called 'Don't Think Twice.' You sound terrific."

For a moment it didn't register.

"Aw, Ellie, thanks for the compliment but that's not me. Remember my friend, Bob Dylan? You met him at the apartment. That's him singing. It's from his new album called 'The Freewheelin.' You should hear the rest of it. It's great."

Bob's facial expression said it all. He got the kick.

"Pete, if you've become that good, Caruso better watch out."

He would later use the Caruso reference regarding himself in a statement he made in 1965.

"I can sing as good as Caruso. I can hit all the notes," he had remarked.

"So, how's school and how are the folks?" he asks in all seriousness.

"Everyone's fine. They miss you. School is different than I

thought, but I'm holding my own. You should see my bottleneck guitar playing now."

He smiles again.

"I miss your folks, too. I'll be down in New York soon so I can make it to say 'Hi.' The schedule Albert (Grossman) set for me has me buffaloed."

"They'd love that."

"By the way," he says, "there's someone I'd like you to meet," as he puts his arm over my shoulder and begins to usher me over to the other side of the room.

There SHE is! This... I never expected THIS to happen. Radiant, beautiful, more attractive than any photo could ever portray her.

"Joanie," he says, "I'd like you to meet a very special friend of mine, Peter McKenzie. You know, the son of the McKenzies. He goes to Harvard. He's always been my biggest fan."

Her face lit up like a Christmas tree as we shook hands.

"I've heard a lot about you and your family, Peter. It's a pleasure to meet you."

Imagine, Joan Baez saying it was actually a pleasure to meet ME? I couldn't think of a cognitive thing to say. Tongue tied and speechless, all I could do was blurt out:

"I'm your biggest fan, too."

They gave each other a knowing glance. Both had broad smiles on their faces. Had they planned this little scene? Bob had just told me he knew I was going to show up and he always got a lift pulling little surprises on me. But this... Joan Baez? There they were, both together talking to Me like there was all the time in the world and no place else they'd rather be.

Bob says:

"You know Joanie's sister, Mimi, is in Cambridge and we hope to be here a couple more days. Maybe we can get together later?"

"That would be terrific," I replied.

The idea was to have a picnic on the bank of the Charles River the next day. That way Ellie could come with me, see Bob again and meet Joan Baez. It was something I looked forward to. Unfortunately, they had to leave sooner than expected for the next city, so the picnic didn't take place. As disappointing as that was there were some mitigating developments. My friends saw I wasn't making it up about knowing Bob Dylan, and for the rest of the semester, in certain circles, I was big man on campus.

(Review in school paper the day after Bob's concert)

BOB DYLAN, a gravel-voiced younger poet of the South and folk hero of bearded teenagers everywhere, opened Jubilee Weekend last night. The dungaree-clad souls of urban hipsters thus satisfied, freshmen turn tonivht to Rock 'n' Roll and the dance. Festivities, featuring DEL SHANNON and HARRY MARSHARD begin at 8 p.m.

(Enlarged photo caption from the school paper the day after Bob's concert)

Now, here it was mid - October 1964, and I was face to face with Suze Rotolo on a Massachusetts sidewalk. We gave each other a hug. She stepped back and studied me.

"So, Peter, how is Harvard treating you?"

"Fine. But what about you? What are you doing here?"

"I live here," she said.

"What, in Cambridge?"

"No, just outside, in Somerville."

"That's fantastic."

Even though I knew she was no longer going out with Bob, I was happy to see her and said without thinking:

"Are you going to Bobby's concert next week?"

"Yes," she replied. "You want to come with me? I have an extra ticket.

"Sure, I do."

"Okay, it's a deal," she affirmed. "Why don't you meet me at my apartment before the concert. We'll catch up and then go together."

She gave me her address. I knew where it was.

That night I gave my two tickets to a female classmate and told her to bring a friend.

On the day of the concert, I arrived on time at Suze's.

"You know," I told her proudly, "since you last saw me my guitar playing has gotten a lot better."

"Really?"

"Yeah. I could show you if we had a guitar."

"Actually, I do," she answered. "It's in the bedroom closet under some clothes."

"You want to hear it right now?"

"Yes," she said.

We went into the bedroom. It was about 10' x 10'. I looked around while she was digging out the guitar to check out her artwork on the walls. There wasn't any. As she pulled the guitar case out I asked:

"Where's your artwork, Suze?"

"Oh, I haven't gotten around to putting it up yet. Are you still painting, Pete?"

"Yes, but not as much as I used to. The academic schedule is intense, and you wouldn't believe the diversity of things I've been exposed to."

"I believe it. Here it is," she said, putting the case on the bed.

I opened it and staring me in the face was one of the great mysteries that has baffled Dylan historians for over 50 years. It was Bob's famous J-50 guitar he used from late 1961 thru late 1963. One day Bob started using another guitar and no one knew what happened to the J-50.

"That's Bobby's guitar," I exclaimed.

"Yes, it is."

While elated, my feelings were divided. Bob had promised me that J-50 back in September 1961. I told Suze the whole story, but quickly added:

"At least it's you, not someone else. You, of all people, deserve it."

I put it on my lap and took the flat-pick from out under the strings. It was a bit out of tune. It didn't sound like the strings had been changed since the last time Bob played it. The action was a little higher than I remembered. I got it in tune and without hesitation played "San Francisco Bay Blues."

"You're getting there, Pete," she said.

[Many years later I met Suze and asked if she still had the guitar. She told me a short time after I played it she'd moved back to New York and it was stolen from her apartment.]

(Bob playing his J-50 guitar)

It was now about 45 minutes before the concert, so it was time to go. We arrived with a few minutes to spare, and you could hear all the pre-concert buzz of voices. A male friend of Suze's, tall, blond, and wearing horned rimmed glasses, met us there and sat on the other side of her. She introduced us. I was restless in my seat. Suze was more laid back. Suddenly, there was a hush, except for the rustling of programs being put away. The house lights started to dim. Suze looked over at me. An overhead spotlight was aimed at the center of the stage. There was a stool off to the side with some harmonicas on it. A light forming a pathway from the side of the stage curtains to the center stage microphone dimmed up and a slight movement of the side stage curtain was noticeable. A boot, a leg and... THERE HE WAS, harmonica holder around his neck, guitar strapped across his shoulders. The place erupted with whistles, applause and shout outs. He strode to the microphone looking confident and completely in charge of what he was going to do. As suddenly as the sound from the crowd had intensified during his entrance, it retreated into complete silence to absorb every one of the verses as...

"Come gather round people wherever you roam..."

blasted all the way up to every corner of the place. Right after the first chorus the big crowd noise went up before the next verse started. He looked dead serious as the words came tumbling out. Whether he had sung that song a hundred times before in 100 different concert halls, the way he was singing it was as if it were the first time, like he discovered it the night before and had only one mission; to pound the point home with a driving, relentless intensity.

He then switched gears and did a great rendition of "Girl From The North Country."

Time passed very quickly, as it always did for me at a Bob concert. Soon it was intermission. As I was about to talk to Suze I noticed her friend seemed agitated. She turned to me.

"Pete, I'm sorry, but my friend and I have to leave. Don't worry, we'll see you later. There's a party where Dick and Mimi Farina are staying. Bob will be there. Come about an hour after the concert ends."

She wrote down the address.

The second half began and after his closing number, the heart breaking "The Lonesome Death of Hattie Carroll," the applause was so long and loud he came back out for an encore. He did "All I Really Want To Do." The audience was laughing every time he sang the chorus. The house lights came on. After exiting and crossing Massachusetts Avenue I glanced back at the outside lights of the theatre and recognized several of my classmates in animated discussions. I looked at the piece of paper Suze had given me.

One hour later I arrived at the written down address. Suze and her friend arrived at the same time. Her friend went inside. She and I remained on the outside stoop. Then I saw it.

"I want to show you something," I said.

She turned and I pointed.

"Look, there's the red dome steeple of my dorm building, Dunster House. It's only two blocks away."

"Wow, that's amazing," she said.

Though no longer a couple it was clear Suze and Bob had continued some type of contact. As the rest of the evening unfolded it became evident there were strong feelings still there, a lot of them unresolved. I was about to ask her what the deal was with this guy she came with...

"Let's go inside," said Suze.

It seemed like things were already in full swing. I was hoping to see Eric Von Schmidt, but he wasn't there. I met Richard and Mimi Farina, though. Suze introduced me to them. As soon as we started to talk someone tapped Richard on the shoulder. He and Mimi turned around and another person grabbed Sue's arm spiriting her away. I was suddenly left standing by myself.

That's when Bob saw me and walked straight over.

"So, how is my favorite Harvard man?"

"Great, Bobby. Do you know my dorm is only two blocks from here and you can see it from the front door?"

"Two blocks, huh?"

Then he asked, "How are your folks?"

"Oh, the same. Only Mom seems to worry that I'm not eating properly, or getting enough sleep."

"Well, if I remember correctly, it IS past your bedtime."

He couldn't resist the tease.

"Well, the times they are a changing," I said back.

It was a good retort by the glint in his eye.

"I see you're wearing a new pair of boots," pointing to his feet.

"Yeah. They've great for performing."

I was dying to tell him about the guitar I had played a few hours earlier and remind him of his forgotten promise to me. Instead, I decided to approach it differently.

"That guitar you were playing tonight…what kind is it?"

He was about to tell me when someone hooked his arm.

"I want you to meet somebody," the someone said.

It looked as if he was almost being dragged.

"We'll talk later, Pete," as his voice receded.

I glanced around and saw Suze across the room talking with her friend from the concert. As I walked over it seemed to me they were more than just friends.

"Do you mind if I talk to Suze alone for a moment?" I asked her 'date.'

"No problem."

"Thanks."

When we got out of earshot I whispered in Suze's ear:

"Does Bobby know about this?"

"No. Why should he?"

"Just curious."

I knew the passion Suze and Bob had had for each other and felt that itchy sense something eventful was going to occur this evening.

Bob had taken their drifting apart, or however you would characterize it, extremely hard. Two and a half years earlier he'd stopped over to the apartment on 28th St. to talk to my mother about Suze taking a solo trip to Italy. He couldn't understand why she wanted to go. He was not happy at all.

"I don't get it," he said.

My mother took the time necessary to give him her analysis.

"Bobby, it's not you. It has nothing to do with you. You're carving out a place for yourself. You have a direction, a goal, and are very focused. Suze has been a big factor in that development. She is younger than you and has yet to establish her own place and direction. She is trying to find her own identity. You've already gone through a lot of those stages. You've broken a few hearts along the way. You must be fair about it. She's not doing this to hurt or abandon you. She loves you. She wants to define how she loves herself."

"But..."

It was the kind of "but" Mom knew was about to expand into a long story. She stopped him.

"Bobby", she continued, "she'll be back. She's not going to be gone forever. In the meantime, concentrate on your work. Think of it as if you're doing that work at an increased pace and imagine she's doing hers in the next room instead of Italy. When you're both back in the same room you'll have that much extra time for play. It will even out."

If anyone could grasp that idea, reconcile and accept it, it was Bob. But, even with his ability to channel feelings of the heart to the brain and out into amazing chains of words for millions of others... not sure he ever did.

And THEN the "eventful" happened... in the Farina's kitchen with Bob opposite Suze's new "friend" and her slightly off to the side. I had never seen Bob in that frame of mind before. He was beyond furious, but still at his intellectual finest, with the words coming so fast it was hard to absorb. Suze was quiet. Every time this fellow tried to respond Bob was one step ahead. The guy may have been smart, but he didn't stand a chance.

"I know exactly what you are starting to say," Bob would interrupt. "It's all fucking bullshit."

He would then go off with another volley of words that would make anyone wilt and become completely voiceless. I could hardly keep up with the speed the words came out. It was clear to me part of him was hurting. It was also the first time I ever heard him use expletives like that. He'd never used them around our apartment, or any other time I was within earshot. Every put down line you've ever heard, could hope to hear, imagine, or couldn't imagine passed his lips. It was nonstop and relentless, like his pounding opening number at the concert earlier. Just as astonishing was the unassailable logic. Then, as suddenly as it started, it stopped. He briefly looked at Suze then walked away. Not once, though, during that time, had he uttered one unkind word about her or to her.

I figured it probably wasn't the best time to restart the conversation with Bob where we'd left off. It could wait. Who knows what could happen next? I decided now was the right time for me to leave. I went over to Suze after a short while and told her I was getting a bit tired and had to get up early and let her know what a great time I had.

"When you see Bobby later, just tell him I had to leave early because it's past my bedtime. He'll understand," I said.

I quietly exited the house. It was nice outside. A slight breeze originating from off the Charles River was in the air. I gazed over and saw the steeple of my dorm building. Five minutes later I was back in my Cambridge home.

CHAPTER 19: A HISTORY LESSON

History fascinated Bob; not just labor, but all world history as far back as you could go. The discussions Bob had with my father during the time he called 28th St. home played a crucial part in his education on that subject. It's obvious in Bob's work approach how closely he listened. Though my father's relation to the union movement and his nonjudgmental approach to people has been previously mentioned, how he processed data is a different issue. If you asked Bob about the effect my father's thought process had on him, he would be the first to say:

"A lot."

Each had natural off the chart intelligence. While both may have had photographic memories, they didn't flaunt it because it wasn't earned. They'd been born with it. What credit can be taken is the ability to disseminate a cogent and insightful analysis of all information acquired. That's the earned. My father had given me some history tips and ways of analyzing things, but he was my dad. I figured he'd always be around so my mind would sometimes wander elsewhere. When I saw how closely Bob and Kevin paid attention when he spoke, I did a complete turnaround. My ears and eyes started immediately attending and observing. It happened bit by bit, day by day.

My father started way back with the Egyptians, Hebrews, Greek philosophers and Roman conquests. His method of analysis served a dual purpose for Bob. It provided him with early validation that he'd already been approaching his music in the most constructive way possible, as well as giving him direction on adapting those methods to other areas of thought.

Hannibal Barker - the great Carthaginian general involved in the second Punic war against the Romans (218-203 B.C.) was a prime example. Completely outnumbered, and without the full support from his native Carthage, he still drove the superior trained Roman armies crazy, defeating them again and again. Hannibal did made mistakes as my father pointed out. He was sometimes impulsive when he shouldn't have been - but he never asked others to do something he himself wasn't prepared to do. That's what marks a real leader. Whatever adverse conditions his troops had to endure Hannibal was right there beside them sharing their discomforts. All we know about Hannibal was written by his enemies. There are no records from his allies, or fellow countrymen. It shows the respect even his most deadly foes had for him. It was all about his strategy, tactics, and attention to detail. He would analyze how his opponents fought and survey the landscape before forming his fight plan. He would determine their weak points and make sure, whenever he could, to occupy the high ground. It was the fluidity of Hannibal's thought process. He garnered all the information he could and then made the requisite adjustments. He never took the position his preconceived plan was best and the facts be damned. Instead, scouring the facts, backgrounds, his opponents' behavioral patterns, he used that knowledge as the foundation for appropriate action. THAT was the key.

My father went through The Middle Ages, The Crusades, The French Revolution, The American Civil War, The Spanish-American War, World War 1, The Russian Revolution, The Spanish Civil War, World War 2, The Korean War… and almost everything in between and current. He always made it clear that others didn't have to come to the same conclusions. The point was to file it away as a reference. Go do your own homework. Take in as much information needed on any individual subject, then make a decision. It may sound like a truism now, but back then, emerging from the 1950's, it was still considered the norm to conform.

The landscape, of course, would not be complete without the inclusion of organized religion and its ever-present tentacles. It was interesting to listen to that part because in Bob, as well as Kevin, you had two full blooded, bar mitzvahed Jewish boys being tutored by a Scotch Presbyterian from Nevada, more versed in Jewish history than the two of them combined. Rather than accept lessons he'd been taught in school, my father's questioning nature led him from an early age to delve into the underpinnings of as many religions as possible. He went through them one by one. While they had different holidays and different ceremonies were their fundamental tenets all that different? One thing he could not stand were those who used religion as a shield to justify certain moral behavior. He was very forceful driving that point home. Put that in the mix and the ever-changing flow of historical events takes on a different meaning. The key to a righteous person is their humanity, not their religion. Again, this was not a widely disseminated point of view at the end of the 1950's. I'm not my father. I can't explain it as well. Whatever Dad was saying Bob assimilated it all.

"How many ears must one man have before he can hear people cry?" is a heck of a thing for a 20-year-old to ask. Maybe "the answer is blowing in the wind" because not enough people ask questions. The shock and horror expressed by many when Bob appeared to enter his born-again Christian routine at the end of the 70's puzzled my father. How else are you going to get answers unless you go to the source?

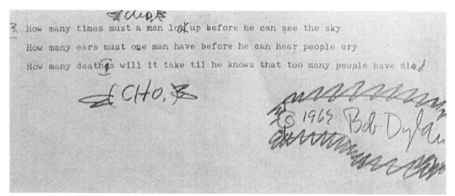

(Bob's original typed lyrics with handwritten corrections)

There was a natural understanding and deep bond between the two of them. It wasn't until later I made one of the connections why Bob had plugged into my father's psyche and why my father spent so much time explaining things.

Bob originally represented himself as being an orphan from the Midwest hopping on freight trains to get from one place to another winding up in the big East Coast City of New York. While we all know now this was not true, the combination of his made-up tales and real background turned out to be the real-life depiction of my father. This was not lost on Bob. As mentioned before, my father, born in 1904, really had been raised in an orphanage, was from a small western mining town, left college at 19, as Bob later would, and headed out to the West Coast City of San Francisco. He hopped freight trains during the Great Depression and didn't look back - at least not for 50 years.

In 1968 I visited Virginia City where my father was born. It was entered on an old steep road called the Geiger Grade, with a vast plain below and mountains in the distance so far away. While I didn't find the orphanage my father had been placed in at the turn of the twentieth century, I stood in front of the small prairie schoolhouse where he had shared lessons with children of all ages.

By standing on the same streets he had as a boy I could physically relate to the trapped isolation and loneliness he must have felt growing up; a sudden and deep visceral connection to him.

Though much of the original town had been demolished and was now mainly a tourist attraction, I could still sense how it had been physically divided, with the stately mansions in one area, and the more rustic houses of the "ordinary folk" in another. Every day, back in my father's time, kids from both sides of town shared the schoolhouse, but outside of school hours the old class system held sway. As a teenager, my father had fallen in love with the wealthy judge's daughter; and she was sweet on him. But, there could be no future in that. This was literally the Old West and being there allowed me to grasp the early roots of my father's political leanings, his passion about equality and his affinity with the American worker– indeed, all working men and women. For him to have remained there, with his great imagination and brain power, would have been unthinkable. In 1922, at the age of eighteen, he got the highest exam scores in the state and enrolled at the University of Nevada.

It may seem odd that the great open spaces of the Mountain West might feel so claustrophobic to a young man, but it all made perfect sense to me. He felt locked down and had to get out and define his own place in the world. My father was the real-life embodiment of the characters who had lived the things that Woody Guthrie and John Steinbeck wrote about, and Pete Seeger sang about. As much as Bob admired Woody and knew all his songs, the impact of a real-life interaction with an actual entity that was a model for many of Woody's characters, and inspired Pete Seeger's voice, was formidable.

There were a couple of specific conversations I remember that really stood out because of the number of changing expressions on

Bob's face while engaged in them. One was when he was talking about the burgeoning civil rights movement as if it were a unique generational thing, only to be informed by my father of the many bloody confrontations down South in the late 1930s, especially in the Louisiana gulf coast ports. They were for the right of NMU Union blacks and whites to share the same sleeping quarters when aboard ship. My father took out his original union membership passbook, which had all the dates stamped in it, illustrating he stationed in the Gulf area while the fight was going on - a first-hand eyewitness account. In the end it was a successful campaign and the NMU became the first union where black-and-white could sleep side-by-side anywhere they shipped out from, or when they were in port on a layover. He finished that conversation by talking about a man he admired. It was Eugene V. Debs, an American Union leader in the late 19th and early 20th century.

Debs was one of the founding members of the Industrial Workers of the World (IWW, or the Wobblies), and five times the candidate of the Socialist Party of America for President of the United States. He was a great orator and Dad had studied his speeches. As he was winding down, he said to Bob in an even tone with great affection:

"Bobby, if you can, remember this. It's from one of Eugene Debs' speeches. I want to pass it on to you. I read it when I was about your age and it stood me in good stead. You don't have to take it literally from a political point of view. Think of it more as an allegory."

Bob leaned forward.

I heard it as well, but could not remember the whole thing. Years later I thought about it and decided to look it up. When I found it, I saw Dad had quoted it exactly, word for word.

"I am not a Labor Leader; I do not want you to follow me or

anyone else; if you are looking for a Moses to lead you out of this capitalist wilderness, you will stay right where you are. I would not lead you into the promised land if I could, because if I led you in, someone else would lead you out. You must use your head as well as your hands, and get yourself out of your present condition."

Bob never forgot it.

Another time Bob was sitting in the kitchen listening to my mother reminisce about her performing background. I hadn't heard these stories before. She explained what life on the road was like as a modern dancer and choreographer in her youth. As she started making a name for herself she began being booked on revue tours around the country, traveling by bus from city to city. The entire show - musicians, dancers, comedians, actors all packed in together. All sorts of people crossed in and about each other. She got to know many of the people from the original Group theater based out of New York. It was a collective formed in 1931 including, among others, Lee Strasburg, John Garfield, Will Geer, Elia Kazan, Lee J. Cobb, Clifford Odets. The group produced and performed many Broadway plays including Golden Boy, Men In White, Waiting For Lefty. The Group was well known and influential back then. Many of the original members went on to become long term icons in the movie and entertainment business. Many of their political views at the time coincided with the ideals my parents believed in and fought for, and were people Bob had heard of, or seen in movies before he came to New York. When my mother mentioned the names, John Garfield and Humphrey Bogart, Bob's eyes got big.

John Garfield was a major leading man in the 1940's, a precursor to the likes of Marlon Brando and James Dean. Humphrey Bogart... no explanation needed.

"You knew Humphrey Bogart and John Garfield?"

"Bogart not that well, Bobby. He was more of an acquaintance. Mac and I were introduced to him at Cafe Society. He seemed like a nice man. It is truly tragic what happened to John Garfield because of the 'Red Scare.' He wouldn't name names and it contributed to his premature death."

She went on to give Bob more insight into the politics of the McCarthy era, as well as a short history of Café Society.

Café Society was a club in the Village that put many entertainers, black and white on the map. It was opened by Barney Josephson in 1938 and closed in 1948. Its unofficial music director was none other than John Hammond. Part of its historical significance is that it was the first entertainment club of its kind that had a complete non segregation policy where black and white sat side by side. It was located at One Sheridan Square.

"That's the same building Suze lives in," Bob would later comment.

"Yes, it was," she answered.

Bob was enthusiastic about "On The Waterfront," the 1955 movie with Marlon Brando. When he talked about Marlon Brando's performance in the film Dad replied:

"Bobby, you are right. Marlon Brando was very good in the role. While the pretext of the movie was dramatically admirable you have to understand, in real life, Brando's character would have been long dead in the first half."

The end of my mother's recollections that night in the kitchen seemed like the coup de gras for Bob. When she told him about having been at the Broadway Paramount Theatre in the 1940s where this young man, Frank Sinatra, whose suit almost looked like it was about to fall off because he was so skinny, you couldn't have pried him away from the table with a crowbar.

"Yes, she said, "that thin young man just oozed sex appeal."

She told him she liked Sinatra in the 1945 short movie "The House I Live In." The movie theme was based on a song of the same title. Bob had seen the film. The music for the song was written by one of her old friends, Earl Robinson, who also wrote the music for the famous song Joe Hill. Joe Hill was a staple in Joan Baez's repertoire. Pete Seeger and Paul Robeson also performed it. Earl wrote "Ballad For Americans" which Paul Robeson originally performed in 1939. Musicians, dancers, artists, singers, actors, writers all intersecting socially and politically with each other.

My father died January 23, 1980, and there was a service for him. Many from all walks of life attended. When one speaker held up a March 24, 1947, copy of Life magazine with an article and my father's picture in it I couldn't help but be reminded that Bob also had a Life magazine piece written about him in 1964.

HOWARD McKENZIE, vice president of maritime union, was one of two who opposed C.I.O.'s anti-Communist resolution.

(Life – March 24, 1947)

(Life – April 10, 1964)

At the end of the service, it was my turn to speak. I chose to read a eulogy/epitaph Howard Harrison, our downstairs neighbor, had written about my father for my mother. The beginning of

Howard's journey began at the same time Jack Elliott first walked into his apartment February 8,1961.

Here is an excerpt...

In him, I saw a flesh and blood
connection to the "America" of
my childhood - the turbulent thirties
and frantic forties. Yes, I've read Hemingway
and Steinbeck and Runyon...
but there was Mac... who could have been
in any of their plots/... and may well have been.

He always encouraged my house
and homebuilding... and cheered my
accomplishments therein - with
the result that I am fearless to
grasp hammer and saw and start again
if ever I must.

And I am not alone in receipt of
his support and approval. Few know
how much you and Mac meant for
the many souls who tramped up the stairs
in the folk days.

No one could have stated it better, or more truthfully.

CHAPTER 20:
ART, ARCHITECTURE,
BUT STILL NO THUMBS

Visual art always intrigued Bob. I started oil painting sophomore year in high school. He was very curious how the paint was applied, what kind of primers were used, how a canvas was stretched, the choice of brushes. Bob did a few drawings while he was with us to see what he could come up with. Sometimes he'd ask me:

"How do you get your ideas for what to paint. How do you decide to put a line here or there? Why did you put the image of the vase on the windowsill rather than the table? Why did you choose that color?"

While I did my best to describe it in technical terms the basic takeaway at the end was "It happens when it happens."

It made perfect sense to me when he said later on:

"Man, I really didn't create those songs. The words were already hanging in the air when I came along. I just knew where to look and transcribe what I saw."

His drawings were not bad. He drew cowboys, guitars and things, as well as little swirls in the margins of some of his lyrics.

Seven years later in June 1968, right after my first year at the Harvard Graduate School of Design in Cambridge, a former college classmate, Hooper Brooks, decided he wanted to go to New York City. He had a car, so I decided to hitch a ride. Thirty minutes out of Cambridge traveling down Massachusetts Turnpike

I tell him, "Hooper, you know Woodstock is on the way to New York. Let's stop there and visit Bob."

He looks at me.

"Bob? Bob who?"

"Bob Dylan."

"You're kidding, right?"

"No, I'm not kidding. You ever been to the Woodstock area?"

"No," he says.

"Since it's not out of our way, why not give it a shot? There's no rush and, at the very least, we'll get to see a nice town."

He thinks for a second. It was his car... a classic Mercedes no less.

"Okay! Why not?"

Now, the only thing I knew was that Bob had a house there somewhere. I had no address, no idea how to get to it once we arrived, or even if he was there at the moment.

Two hours later we pull into the town. It's basically one long main drag with little shops, restaurants, bed and breakfast places surrounded by hundreds of square miles of treetops and unmarked dirt roads. We look at each other and think the same thing:

"Post office!"

We find the one small post office for the whole area. It's on Main Street and it's open. We look for the supervisor. We find him.

"Pardon me," I ask. "We have a question."

"Shoot," he says.

"I'm an old friend of Bob Dylan and we thought we'd drop by and pay him a visit."

He looks me in the eye. It was a slow day, so he had time to take a measure of me. He looks me up and down. Then he looks Hooper up and down.

"Oh, Bob. Yeah, he comes in here sometimes to get his mail."

"That makes sense," I say, "but we were hoping you could give us directions to his house."

"His house, his house," he mutters to himself. "Tell you what," as he steps outside with us and points. "Drive to the end of Main Street. That's where the dirt roads start."

"Then, what?"

"Can't help you there," he says.

"But it's hundreds of square miles of trees."

"As I said," he repeats, "drive to the end of Main Street. That's where the dirt roads start."

It is obvious that's all we are going to get. We walk out and get back in the car and drive all the way down Main Street to the very end where the backwoods roads begin, and the hundreds of square miles of trees are. Go left, right, or forget about it? Left sounds good. We arrive at a fork in the road. We go right. As we drive there are turn offs here, there, everywhere. We are over a mile down that road. There's another unmarked turn off on the right.

"Turn here," I say to Hooper.

"Why here?"

"Seems as good a place as any."

We are driving down a very bumpy, narrow path. After a couple hundred feet you can't see the main road anymore. We drive a bit more. Maybe we should turn around...

Suddenly, the road gets wider and there's a clearing. I'm sitting on the passenger side. Down a sloping area are 1, 2, 3... 5 cars.

I had heard that several musicians who worked with Bob during his tours lived in the area and had decided to form their own, independent band. If this was their house maybe they could help us out. What's the worst that could happen?

We stop, turn off the engine and get out of the car. It's very quiet, except for the natural sound of the woods and chirping of the birds.

There's a modest size house, nothing fancy. Fifty to a hundred feet in front of it is a low rock wall with a 4-foot wide opening and a couple of steps leading down into the front yard. While we debate going down the steps to knock on the front door, we hear a noise on the house's far side. Around the corner emerges this figure. He must have heard the car engine in the driveway. It's the only time I think I've ever seen Bob so startled. It took him a moment to say something.

"Pete, what are you doing here?"

He kept walking toward us.

"How'd you find me?"

"Plain dumb luck," I replied.

I hadn't seen him since before he went to London in 1966 and wasn't quite sure what to expect; mod outfits, high-heeled boots, big hairdo, the sometimes distant look in his eye you see in films of him from then? I hadn't yet seen or heard his 1967 "John Wesley Harding" album. As he came closer, I saw he was wearing sandals and similar clothes and hat to what he is wearing on the cover of his later 1969 album, "Nashville Skyline." His jacket was seersucker. He had shortish hair and the same type of almost beard and mustache as on that cover.

"How've you been, Pete?" he said with a firm handshake.

"Fine. By the way, this is my friend, Hooper Brooks. He's a friend from school. We're on our way to visit my parents."

"Nice to meet you, Hooper."

Another handshake.

Hooper later remarked how light Bob's hand felt when he shook it. No surprise there. The first time I shook Bob's hand it was the same thing. I guess the longer he knows and trusts you the firmer the grip, or else he's just protecting his hand.

As we started talking, it was the same affable 28th St. Bob, like no time had passed and some instinctive trigger had been switched on. Sure, I had been through my own personal experiences and growth... and so had he. He was married, now a father a couple times over, but it didn't appear to have changed the basic, interpersonal mechanic between us. Right out of the gate he asked:

"How are Eve and Mac?"

"They're fine and they miss you."

I asked him how he liked living in the country.

It's fine," he said, "but, don't people get it? Man, I wish people would leave me alone. If I wanted to deal with them I'd still be living back in the city. They won't go away on their own."

Rather than pursue that subject I changed it.

"What about The Byrds and "Mr. Tambourine Man? I asked.

"Ah, that," he said with a laugh and then he, too, changed the subject.

He was pleased I'd graduated college and ended my first year of graduate school on my way to becoming an architect.

Except for "The Byrds" inquiry, music talk was a very minor part of the conversation. He told us how he liked London and how he'd become friendly some people over there.

"And what about you?" Bob asked Hooper.

Hooper explained his interest in city planning and his concern with the shrinking amount of green space within modern cities.

Bob was quite interested in what Hooper was saying, picking up on his high intelligence. I told Bob I was planning to go out to Los Angeles later in the summer to stay with my cousins, Larry and Leslie.

"How're they doing?"

"Great. Their business has really expanded. That's why they're out there."

"Send them my regards."

"I will. After, I may go up to San Francisco to see Duke and Millie."

"Hey, that's great. You know I always liked them a lot."

I thought for a moment about Avril in San Francisco but decided best not to bring it up.

"So, Pete, what about your art?"

The way he said it was not just because he was interested. He knew me well enough to know I was dying to tell him about it.

"I'm glad you asked. In fact, why don't I show you some," I answered. "I have a whole bunch of drawings in the car. It's a different style than I was doing before."

I'd been into huge murals, sort of in the Matisse vein, and one night I took a break. I started idly drawing and the beginning of this new style was staring at me from the page.

"I'll be right back," I said, as I started toward the car to rummage through the backseat.

I came back out with several pieces. I always felt good about sharing my artwork with Bob because it was one area he would never attempt to challenge me on. He had no problem asking questions, though. This time was no different. He studied each piece and then went back to one drawing. That one had a gesturing figure standing on a small free-floating sphere in space. He looked at me, looked back at the picture and asked in his sincerest tone:

"Pete, there is one thing I don't quite understand. How did you manage to get a person to pose for you on a ball in the middle of the air like that? How does that work?" For a split second I was going to answer him. He'd done it again. Caught me up short. Some things never do change. It was like the card tricks all over again. He couldn't resist the little tease.

"Aw, c'mon now, stop that," I answered.

But, the deed was done. He knew he'd gotten me for that split second.

"You know," he said, "I've been doing some painting and drawing myself. I just did the artwork for the cover of an album the guys that backed me up touring recorded. They decided to put out a record as an independent, self-contained group. They call themselves 'The Band'."

"'The Band'?" I exclaimed. You mean name of the band they formed is called 'The Band'?"

"Yeah, that's the name. Just 'The Band.' We did a lot of jamming up here together and they decided to do a solo turn. It should be out in about a month. It'll be my painting on the cover."

"That's really great," I replied. "You're branching out into an area that always had your heart."

Bob was very proud of it.

He went back to looking at my drawings. When he was through he looked at me with a slight nod of the head letting me know he liked what he saw.

Before we knew it over an hour had gone by and there was still a way to go to get to New York City before all the traffic congestion. While there were many other things I wanted to talk to him about it could wait for another time. Besides, maybe he had some other things of his own he had to do.

I gathered up the drawings.

"It was nice to meet you," Bob said to Hopper.

"It's nice to meet you, too, Mr. Dylan."

"Call me Bob. Any friend of Pete's is a friend of mine."

Walking back to the car Hooper remarked:

"You know, Pete, he's nice, well-mannered, and a well-spoken person. It was a pleasant surprise. I didn't have a clue what to expect."

As our car pulled out I gave a last look through the rear window as Bob was walking back to the house before he was cut off from view by the trees. When we hit the main road I turned to Hooper.

"Do you think Bob is wondering right now, "How the heck did Pete and his friend find me?"

(Cover painting by Bob Dylan for The Band's first album -1968)

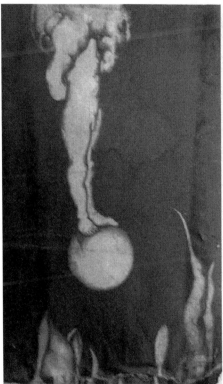

(The drawing Bob teased me about)

CHAPTER 21: HIJINX IN JULY

As July 1961 progressed things were routine around the apartment. Bob came and went, making new friends, and sometimes bringing them up to the apartment to see how my folks would react. More guitar lessons.

One evening a group of people, mostly friends of my parents, gathered at the apartment. It was a nice social get together. Bob was there. During the chatter the subject turned to Bob. They all knew him in one form or another and liked him. But then, some started giving their unsolicited advice on his appearance and his wardrobe. They weren't putting him down - just trying to be helpful because they thought they knew better.

"Kid, you've got a lot of talent, but you dress like a vagabond with your wrinkled clothes and your hair messy. If you want to make the right impression you should put on a jacket and tie like some of those other clean-cut looking kids and comb your hair. People will take you more seriously. You're a nice-looking young man and you should dress appropriately," one said.

I was surprised by the ferocity of my mother's immediate response. The firmness with which she spoke gained everyone's attention.

"First of all, while I know you mean well on Bobby's behalf, you have no real idea how show business works. His clothes are always clean. That's always made sure of. If they're wrinkled it's on purpose. It's his choice. I could iron the clothes anytime he wants, but he doesn't want that. If his clothes seem mismatched it's not because he has no taste. It's done on purpose. He is very conscious of the image he presents. That's why he does it. He has a plan. He's his own man and I, for one, agree with it. He is doing just fine, thank you. He knows exactly what you're saying and has made a conscious decision not to dress up like men in suits. It's absolutely the wrong time for him to dress like a prep schoolboy. And don't even think about making a comment on his cap. One day, though, I predict, you will see him not only wearing a suit, but a tuxedo. Just not now."

That put a clamp on any further comments, or discussion of Bob's wardrobe and hairstyle. He remained silent the entire time, not involving himself in the matter. When everyone finally left Bob turned to her.

"Thank you, Eve."

She stopped what she was doing, went over to him, gave him a kiss on the cheek.

"You're doing fine just the way you are."

An extra big smile crossed his face.

While it was always nice when he smiled, he wasn't smiling a few days later - at the Fifth Avenue Hotel - 5th Avenue and 11th St., the upscale part of Greenwich Village. At least, not initially.

Kevin had booked Bob to appear at an evening function there figuring it would be a good chance to get him exposed to a slightly different crowd of people. You never know who might be in the audience. Mom, Dad, Bob, Kevin and I all piled into a cab. Kevin was paying. Bob was dressed as Bob. Kevin was dressed in a sharkskin suit and tie. I was wearing a pair of khakis and a dress shirt. My parents were appropriately attired as older people are.

The taxi speeds 17 blocks down to the hotel.

We all get out and enter the lobby. The performing ballroom is off to the right. Kevin checks in to let them know Bob has arrived as we all head toward the main room. On our way in a man brushes past us on his way out. As soon as we get through the ballroom doorway Bob says to my mother:

"You don't like the man that just passed us."

"Why would you say that?" my mother asks him with a surprised look.

"The slight stiffening of your spine as he walked by..."

"You're right, Bobby. I don't like him."

The fellow hadn't recognized my mother. I suspect the dislike had to do with some incident involving my father's union activities years before. Bob, as usual, was the eagle-eyed observer.

We are all in the ballroom. What a scene. Not only were almost all the people there aged from their mid-40's to mid-60's, but the men were dressed in what appeared to be Jackie Gleason like Raccoon Lodge outfits, all chattering away with their wives at different tables. They filled the entire room. You could almost sense Lawrence Welk hiding behind a curtain with his orchestra all squeezed beside him against the wall, waiting to explode out into the open as soon as the cue was given. There was a tiny little stage in the middle of the far end of the packed space. It appeared Kevin had either been misinformed about the venue crowd, or had been given the wrong date; there was no indication, or even a notation when Bob was supposed to go on. This was a pickle and Bob wasted no time letting him know it.

"Kevin, what have you gotten me into?"

Fortunately, at that moment, Jack Elliott, guitar case in hand, enters the lobby looking for us. Bob must have told him about the booking and asked him to come down. I was glad to see him. Given the circumstances Bob was even gladder. At least there was an addition to deal with this unexpected turn of events and Jack had that laid-back way about him that could put anyone at ease.

"What a crowd we've got here, huh? Look at 'em. We can have some fun," he says.

Some of the edge immediately comes off Bob.

"Aw, what the hell," Bob replies.

They both notice the bar at the same time.

"We'll be back in a bit."

I'm left watching their two guitars.

"Where's Kevin?" I ask Mom and Dad.

Whoever came up with the term where there's two there's three had it right. Kevin had already beaten Bob and Jack to the 80% proof area.

Dad shrugs his shoulders.

"Young folks."

One act goes on, then some speaker starts talking. I wasn't paying particular attention. After a while Kevin comes back from the bar a bit more loquacious than usual. 45 minutes have passed since we had entered the hotel.

"Kevin, how many drinks did you have?" Mom asks him.

I notice my father's bemused expression.

"Don't worry, Eve," Kevin replies with a lopsided smile.

It's the first time I'd seen Kevin in that state.

"But Bobby and Jack, what about...?"

She didn't have time to finish because Jack and Bob come strolling back over. Strolling is an approximate description.

"Hey, Eve, everything okay?" Bob asks, giggling.

Jack is right beside him. It's obvious why all three of them had spent so much time at the bar. I was, as yet, unfamiliar with the word "tanked." Bob and Jack look over at the stage which was temporarily unoccupied.

"What do ya think?" says Jack to Bob

"Now might be a good time," Bob answers.

Both look at me.

"Guitars, please."

As they are opening their guitar cases Kevin is making his way to the stage and microphone.

"Good evening, ladies and gentlemen. I'm here to present to you a couple of very special talents who will soon be big stars. C'mon up here, boys. And to all you folks sitting here tonight, give 'em a really big round of applause."

He sounded like Ed Sullivan with a rolled-up pack of cigarettes in his tee shirt.

"After you," says Bob to Jack.

"No, after you," says Jack to Bob.

"Okay," Bob replies.

The two of them start weaving through the tables to get to that little stage; weaving in the broadest sense of the word. Both are now on that little platform tapping the mike to make sure it's still working.

"Hello," says Jack. "My name is Jack... "

I couldn't make out exactly how he pronounced his last name.

"And this here is my friend, Bob Dylan. We're here to specially entertain you. Ready, Bob?"

"Yup."

They must have discussed what to do over at the bar, or more likely, on their way up to the stage. It was a carefully planned 'fly by the seat of the pants operation.' I don't remember exactly how many songs they did, but their exchanges back and forth in between numbers had me in stitches. I know THEY were having fun. And Jack HAD been completely honest with the audience. They'd lived up to their promise. Their performance certainly was "special."

There was a slight smattering of polite applause when they were done and stepped off the stage.

"How'd it go?" said Bob to my mother.

"I think it's time for everyone to go home."

"But the night's just starting," he went on.

"No," answered Mom. "The night has ended and we're going home."

I didn't see Kevin anywhere. Jack decided to ramble off into the night as Bob, Mom, Dad and I headed back to the apartment.

The next morning Bob got up a bit later than usual. Except for his hair sticking up he looked and talked the same as he always did.

"That was some night last night. How do you feel today, Bobby?" Mom asked as she was getting breakfast ready.

"Fine. It was no big deal."

Later in the day, when he met up with Kevin, Kevin didn't get the same polite answer.

By the middle of the month, I went down to perform at the Washington Square fountain by myself. Having gone down once before to play with Kevin, I figured I was musically passable enough to go alone. Bob had taught me a few more things. I mean, there were people down there that literally couldn't hold a tune or play more than two chords. There were always a couple also a couple of clubs you could go to on a Sunday afternoon that let anyone get up and perform. I decided on the club option. There was a nice, quiet place near Bleecker and MacDougal Street. It had a fair size stage with daylight coming through the street window. There were only a few patrons at the tables. Sitting off to the side of the stage I didn't have to wait long. There were not a lot of names on the sign-up sheet. Soon, it was my turn.

"Hello, my name is Peter McKenzie and I'm going to do a couple of songs for you. Hope you like them."

I did the first song, playing it a little faster than normal. That happens when you're nervous. There were one or two claps and then a raspy voice, not too loud, in the back, talking to a friend of his:

"Who does this kid think he is, Bob Dylan?"

The tone in his voice didn't quite sit right with me, but I thought to myself, "At least he knows who Bob is. That's a good thing."

I ignored the comment and began my next number. This time, however, there is no waiting until the second song was over. A running commentary started from this guy.

"That kid doesn't look like Bob Dylan..."

That did it. Rather than endure his heckling, I left out a couple of verses and cut the song short.

"Thank you very much," I said and got offstage.

I packed up the guitar as the next performer was getting ready and couldn't wait to get out of that place. I wanted to give the heckler a piece of my mind, but he was a big guy so I just kept silent and left. When I got home I told my parents and Bob what happened while describing the heckler.

The following Wednesday evening we are sitting in the living room when Bob comes in the front door.

"I've brought a friend I want you to meet," he says.

His friend walks through the door and his facial expression does an about face.

"It's you!" the friend exclaims when he sees me.

I say nothing.

He stammers:

"Listen, kid, I'm really sorry. Had I realized who you were I would never have said any of the things at the club the other afternoon. I'd have asked you over to our table."

Bob is off to the side.

"Oh, I see since you two have already met so you don't need an introduction. Eve and Mac, this is Dave Van Ronk."

That was our formal introduction. In the end Dave turned out to be a real sweetheart. He was a big rough bear of a man, but a real softy. I got to like him a lot. I've often wondered if Dave told Bob beforehand about the kid at the club. If he did had Bob put things together and decided to have some fun at Dave's expense? It would be in character. Whatever the backstory, the expression on the great Dave Van Ronk's face...

CHAPTER 22: HAROLD LEVENTHAL

Harold Leventhal was one of the biggest folk promoters around, and occasional manager. He came from a poor family, but always loved music and started in the business being a song plugger for Irving Berlin, the composer who wrote "God Bless America." As Mr. Leventhal grew older he branched out to promoting concerts for various left wing and union causes. He promoted The Weavers, Pete Seeger, Cisco Houston, Joan Baez, The Clancy Brothers. He helped promote fundraisers for the Abraham Lincoln brigade: the division of American volunteers that fought against Franco in the Spanish Civil War in the 1930's. Many of them later joined the National Maritime Union. Subsequently, he worked with artists such as Johnny Cash, Harry Belafonte, Judy Collins and Neil Young. He was also the business manager for Woody Guthrie. After Woody died in 1967, he virtually adopted Woody's son, Arlo. He produced the movie "Alice's Restaurant." Woody Guthrie couldn't stand "God bless America" and in protest he wrote "This Land is Your Land," possibly THE most patriotic American song ever. Along with Woody's daughter, Nora, he established the Woody Guthrie foundation to preserve Woody's legacy.

Right after the first week in July, while Bob was out and about, my father, who was talking to Kevin and me says:

"Why don't I give Harold Leventhal a call and see if we can't have him do something for Bobby? From what I gather he's now well established and respected in the folk world."

He looks up Harold's phone number and calls his office. Mr. Leventhal's secretary picks up the phone.

"Hello," says my father, "if Harold is in can you tell him Howard McKenzie is on the line."

"Hold on a minute, sir. I'll see if he's available."

About 30 seconds later there is a click and a voice says:

"Hello, Mac, how are you? It's been a long time."

I can hear the other side of the conversation because my ear is right next to my father's. Kevin is sitting across the room.

"I'm doing ok, Harold. Eve's fine. Our son, Pete, is now in high school. He's a fine artist."

They talk a bit about their former union days, the House Un-American Activities Committee, Woody Guthrie, the blacklisting of Pete Seeger...

"I sometimes hear your name bandied about," Dad says. "You've done some good things for good people."

"Well, Mac, it's a living."

"Listen, Harold, I know your position in the folk music community. I wouldn't normally do this, but this is a very special situation and I wanted to contact you first. You have some time to talk?"

"For you, Mac, sure. I'm listening."

"Harold, we have a young man who is staying with us from the Midwest. He's been in town about six months. He's a folksinger who's extremely talented with real potential. He's writing his own material. If you heard him you might be interested."

"What's his name?"

"Bob Dylan"

"Name vaguely rings a bell. Does he have a tape, or anything else I could listen to?" Harold asks.

"Give me a minute to find out. You know Gerde's Folk City?"

"Of course," he says.

"He recently completed a two-week paying engagement there with John Lee Hooker and they really liked him. Hold on a second and let me check about a tape."

Dad puts his hand over the speaker so Harold can't hear and asks Kevin if he has any tapes of Bob.

"Yes," says Kevin.

My father takes his hand off the speaker.

"There is a tape."

"Good," says Harold. Why don't you send it over and I'll listen to it. After I do I'll get right back to you. You know my address?"

"I believe so, but give it to me yourself to make sure it's correct."

Harold gives him the address.

"Just mark it 'Personal' so the staff knows to give it to me as soon as it arrives."

"All right, Harold."

After a little more talk my father hangs up.

The next day a copy of the tape is sent to Mr. Leventhal's office.

Harold was true to his word. As soon as he got the tape, with a short note enclosed, he listened and got back immediately. I don't know if he checked around to get any input on Bob, but his response was not the one hoped for.

"The young man is very interesting. Unfortunately, with the number of people I'm handling I can't take on someone else right now. But, definitely good luck to him."

It was a gentlemanly way of saying he wasn't interested.

However, all's well that ends well. Less than two years later he was approached by Bob's management team to promote Bob's first New York City solo concert at Town Hall April 12,1963. He did it, and then followed up six months later with the next major Bob Dylan solo concert at Carnegie Hall on October 26, 1963.

Although Harold did present Bob's first solo concert at Town Hall, it wasn't the first time Bob had performed there. On October 5, 1962, he was part of a hootenanny where several other acts performed. He got a feel for the whole ambience of the venue in front of a live audience without having the pressure of the entire spotlight on him; like a dress rehearsal.

It was also the first time I saw Ian and Sylvia perform.

Kevin and I were sitting next to each other. He couldn't take his eyes off Sylvia; the way she moved her leg when she sang. When the concert ended Kevin said:

"I'm going backstage. I want to meet that singer, Sylvia."

I wanted to go backstage to see Bob. Before we could, Bob happened to come walking out to the orchestra area by himself.

"I'm going to go backstage and meet Sylvia," Kevin said.

Bob looked at Kevin and moved slightly to the right, partially blocking the steps up to the stage that led to the dressing room. He knew the score. Ian and Sylvia were his friends, and also a couple.

"Kevin, I don't think now would be a good time. It's pretty crowded back there."

He caught Bob's meaning right away. Kevin didn't get to meet Sylvia.

The first time Bob was on the Carnegie Hall stage was September 22, 1962. He was part of a hootenanny with Pete Seeger and several others.

His solo concert there was just over a year later.

It happened the same way at Forest Hills Tennis Stadium. Bob made a guest appearance courtesy of headliner, Joan Baez, August 17, 1963.

That was two years before August 28, 1965.

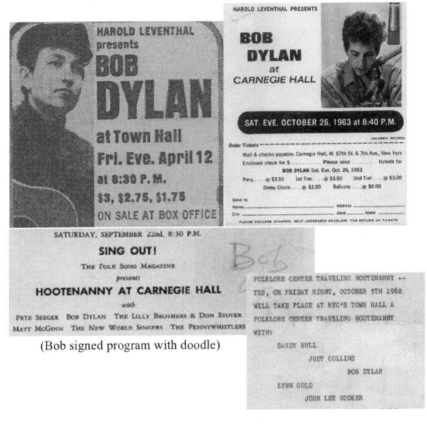

(Bob signed program with doodle)

JOAN BAEZ SINGS AT FOREST HILLS; 14,700 Hear Her and Bob Dylan in Folk Concert New Songs in Repertory

CHAPTER 23:
AN ADDITION TO THE SHIP'S CARGO MANIFEST

On August 28, 1965, Bob Dylan was the headline solo act at Forest Hills Tennis Stadium in Queens, New York. His 5th album, "Bringing It All Back Home," had already come out. Electric amps were flowing through some of the grooves on the record. His 6th album, "Highway 61 Revisited," hadn't yet been released. Bob liked to shock people to wake them up, not PUT them in shock. As always with him it was still about the words; the music and arrangements were always done in a way to reinforce the words to make them more forceful and effective.

The security was intense. Unlike other Dylan concerts where you could sit right up front of the stage, the lawn area in front was devoid of chairs and cordoned off. If you managed to avoid security and sprinted across the field to try and reach it, there were guards stationed to stop your momentum.

The place started filling up. It was an open roofed stadium where you could see the night sky. 15,000 people were in the stands. An announcement was being made on the stage and suddenly, just like that, Bob was standing at the microphone in front of this huge mass of humanity.

What a figure he cut! Unlike four years earlier, now WAS the right time to be dressed a certain way. He wasn't wearing a tie, but he WAS wearing a beautifully tailored dark suit, white striped shirt with cufflinks and a tie pin through the buttoned collar; his pair of black ankle boots firmly planted, the acoustic version of "She Belongs To Me" rang throughout the stadium. While I had my own focus, cheering as loud as I could, it was hard to clearly hear the overall applause he always got. Maybe the wind was diluting it. He went through some of his more recent compositions acoustically. The one that got me was new.

I'd already heard a little bit about the song, "Desolation Row." Months earlier, during the recording of Bob's soon to be released new record, "Highway 61 Revisited," his producer, Bob Johnston, came to our apartment to see my parents. He brought with him some of the lyrics Bob had written for inclusion on the record. The purpose of his visit was to get some insight and advice on how best interact with Bob. After all, who would know better than Eve and Mac McKenzie. It was a little reserved at first. They had never met before. My parents told him:

"You're the expert in sound. You know more than we do. Just be yourself. Don't try to be anyone else and you'll get along fine."

They liked him.

My parents told me about this one lyric starting with something about postcards and hanging. They thought it was remarkable. When he started to sing "They're selling postcards of the hanging" ... I knew it was the song they were referring to.

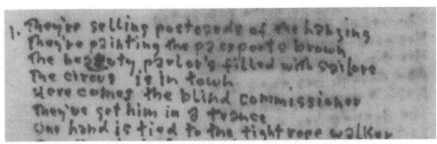

(Handwritten lyrics to "Desolation Row")
-From the William Pagel archives-

It had to be the longest song he ever wrote. But the words… I'm glad his new album came out two days later so I could listen to it several times over. It was a masterpiece of imagery. There was no dilution of sound from the wind this time. The crowd's hands were like one long drawn-out thunderclap.

After two more acoustic numbers, Intermission...

The second half started. I couldn't believe it. From what I was able to hear the nays seemed to equal the yays as Bob opened with a new song called "Tombstone Blues," backed by a full electric band. Why the antipathy in the crowd? They were already familiar with "Bringing It All Back Home," and half that album was electric. If they didn't like him playing electric, why had they bothered to show up? They had to know, if they'd followed Bob's music in the slightest, he wasn't going to stop exploring boundaries. He'd already given them an incredible acoustic first half. "Desolation Row," alone was worth the price of admission. This was music with a very carefully thought-out purpose; to put the right backbone to the words of each song, showcasing them in their most potent form. Bob didn't play electric to drown out, or mask the words because they weren't up to his usual par. That wasn't part of his work ethic.

A version of "I Don't Believe You" and a new song, "From A Buick Six," followed.

When his new composition, "Just Like Tom Thumb's Blues," echoed in the night air, the combination of the words with the electric arrangement...

This was not 'standard' Rock 'n Roll. The style of music combined with his unrivaled grasp of words created an atmosphere of mystery and fog, enveloping and whisking you away to a completely new place of adventure. The booing puzzled me. If they felt the words to any song were clunkers, that would have been one thing. That wasn't the case. To those paying attention, it was evident he had a very carefully constructed set order worked out. He had a strategy, but like Hannibal, the Carthaginian general, it was his tactics that made it work.

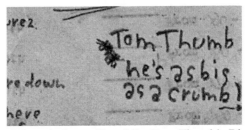

(Detail from lyrics to "Just Like Tom Thumb's Blues")
-From the William Pagel archives-

Bob next did "Maggie's Farm" from his previous album. It brought the crowd back into more familiar territory.

He followed up with "It Ain't Me Babe," which the 'folk crowd' always loved. Even though backed by a band, doing an older, familiar standard temporarily brought the crowd a bit more back into the fold. Yet, he'd been steadily making clear, even if they hadn't caught on, it wasn't that the "Old" Bob had already left the building, he hadn't even entered it.

After Bob did a little fiddling around on the keyboards the sound of another new electric number, "Ballad Of A Thin Man," was pouring through the stadium speaker system.

The audience seemed to have lost much of its negativity.

Then there was THAT number…

While it was to be included on the "Highway 61 Revisited" album which hadn't come out yet, "Like A Rolling Stone" had been released as a single a month earlier. It was not unfamiliar to a large portion of the crowd and had been climbing the Billboard 100 chart where it eventually wound up as the #2 most popular song in the nation. Now it is considered by many to be the #1 rock song of all time. People were even joining in on the chorus.

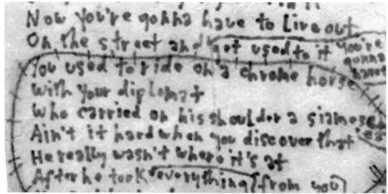

(Handwritten lyrics with corrections from "Like A Rolling Stone")

Then it was over. No backstage visit or milling around. After the last drum beat Bob is spirited away, his band following.

As my parents and I get up and the gargantuan audience starts to dissipate I hear this voice:

"Peter."

I look around and about 100 feet away is Suze Rotolo. I turn to my parents:

"Hey, there's Suze."

They see her and wave. She waves back. Being nimble I sprint over, sidestepping one person after another, almost bowling her over with my momentum when I reach her. She laughs.

"Boy, you are full of energy," she says.

"Yeah, some night."

"I thought you were in Cambridge. You are what, a junior now?" she asks.

"Not quite. I will be in about three weeks when the semester starts. I've been working in Cambridge for the summer and came down today specially for this. I have to take the train back tomorrow afternoon."

I hadn't seen Suze since that October night in 1964. That was only 10 months ago, but...

"It's insane," she says reflectively. "This is a true madhouse. It's crazy. 15,000 reacting every which way. And the vastness of the space. People getting dragged off the stage. The music is great, but I'm really not sure I would want, or could handle all the fame and craziness that seem to go with it."

I understood what Suze meant. Even if they had still been a couple how could she do her art and deal with all the pressure and blistering performance scheduling Bob was under? He would want her with him the whole time. While he could see several moves ahead in a chess game, so could she. Many things I'd not quite understood before now made sense.

It was time for everyone to go home. It happened to be a bit chilly for an August night, and from the audience viewpoint, despite the patches of positives, it had seemed not to have been the warmest of receptions.

I was told a story years later which came from Harvey Brooks, the bass player in Bob's band that night. He explained how everyone went back to Albert Grossman's place after the show. They all acknowledged that because of the empty lawn area in front of the stage, and the bright lights in their eyes, no one could really see the audience. All of them were positioned near the foot speakers so they could hear each other play. Because of that, and the open air dissipating the spectator noise, hearing the crowd was difficult. As they sat around Albert's apartment Bob said:

"I think it went pretty well tonight, boys."

At another concert on October 1, 1965, at Carnegie Hall in New York City, a scenario occurred I never knew the full details of until Don Scardino, whom I hadn't seen in over 40 years, recently filled me in. He's a former actor, based in Hollywood, now a successful TV and movie director. He's a couple years younger than I. I met him in the early 1960's because he was the boyfriend of my mother's former dance protégé. Mom, to help make ends meet, had returned to her own roots by teaching modern dance techniques to students at my elementary school in the late 1950's. I asked him if he'd bumped into Bob out there.

"No, I never ran into him."

"That's a shame", I replied.

"But, we did get to meet."

"You did?"

He began to describe it...

'Your mother had taken Connie and me to see Bob's concert at Carnegie Hall in late 1965. We were all backstage before the show. Suddenly, the backstage hands told everyone to clear the area because Bob was about to arrive. They began ushering everyone out. When they approached us Eve said, "But, I'm his foster mother."

She winked at us to play along.

"Ok Ma'am, we understand. You can stay, but you have to wait over there," said the stage manager.

Within a couple of minutes Bob came down the corridor followed by members of his band. Out of the corner of his eye he caught a glimpse of your mother.

"Hold up a sec," he said to everyone.

He walked right over to your Mom and gave her a kiss. I couldn't hear the words exchanged between them, but she turned and said:

"Bobby, I want you to meet two young friends of mine. They're big fans."

"Sure, Eve."

She introduced us to him.

"It's a pleasure to meet you both, especially since you are friends of Eve's."

He couldn't have been more gracious. Still smiling, looking at your mother, he said:

"Gotta get ready for the show."

"Was he wearing sunglasses?" I asked Don.

"He took them off when he came over to your mother.'"

Three weeks after his October 1, 1965 appearance at Carnegie Hall Bob was in Boston at the Back Bay theatre. It's one of his Boston area performances I missed. My Harvard friend, Eric Herter, was there that night. The main difference between Forest Hills and that concert was the circumstance.

By October 25, Bob's album, "Highway 61 Revisited," had been out for two months and given people more time to get acclimated to the "new" sound. The crowd feedback was very positive. The first half was solo and completely acoustic. When the intermission was over the curtain parted and the stage was bathed in red light. The band, all dressed in black, with Bob at the piano, kicked off with the electric "Ballad of A Thin Man." He hadn't really talked in between numbers, but as he was about to exit the stage at the end of the show he said into the microphone:

"Sorry I didn't talk in between songs, but I just recovered from a slight case of leprosy."

Normally when he made a wisecrack it would zing into the crowd without a hitch. This time was different.

He was standing out in front of the band. The tech in charge of making sure the heavy front stage curtains closed on time must have been a bit nervous because he closed them a fraction too soon. Just after Bob said "leprosy" the curtains came together knocking him off balance. He didn't fall, but he never used the word "leprosy" in a careless manner again.

(Inscribed page by Bob from
Daniel Kramer's book, "Bob Dylan")

CHAPTER **24**:
THE ORIGINAL CARGO MANIFEST

Many people who have studied Bob over the years have called the August 28, 1965, Forest Hills concert his most important big, live performance. In my opinion, Bob's most important big, live performance took place a little over two years earlier on July 26, 1963, the first night of the Newport Folk Festival in Newport, Rhode Island. It was an event that happened once a year where all the best folksingers, blues players, bluegrass groups came from all over to perform on the main stage throughout 3 afternoons and 3 nights. In addition, there are side workshops, more intimate, where you get to see many of the performers up close and even talk with some.

On Tuesday afternoon, July 23, 1963, Kevin was sitting in our apartment. Since Bob was going to play at Newport that year he intended to drive up to the festival to see him.

"When do we leave?" I invited myself.

"Hm, let's see," he said. "It starts this weekend and goes for three days. We could leave early Friday afternoon and catch the first night's performance."

In the late afternoon, Friday, July 26, 1963, Kevin, myself and Mark Eastman climbed into Kevin's car. Mark had been with Bob and Kevin the first time Bob had arrived in NYC in January 1961 and was also with them the first time Bob visited Woody Guthrie in the hospital. Bob liked him.

Three hours later we arrived at our destination. Kevin had been there on previous occasions. Once we got off the highway he had no trouble finding the festival parking. You just parked your car as near as possible to where the main stage was. We got lucky and found a space just outside the area marked off where the audience was supposed to sit or stand.

It was twilight when we got out of the car. The crowd was large, and the stage spotlights had been turned on.

"Did Bob Dylan play yet?" I asked the first person I saw.

"Not yet, man. I hear he's coming on later."

The festival included the big names - Joan Baez, Pete Seeger, Judy Collins, Brownie McGee and Sonny Terry, Jack Elliott, Peter, Paul and Mary and many others. Kevin and Mark were chatting when I told them I was going to get as close to the stage as possible. The sun had finally set so I had to be careful where I stepped. Eventually, I got within 25 feet of the stage, slightly off to the left side center. It was a perfect view. I wasn't tired from the drive, and even though I hadn't eaten dinner I didn't feel the least bit hungry. I wasn't paying close attention to the performers that went on over the next two hours. I was looking around to see if I could recognize anyone I might know. Then, over the stage speakers:

"... Bob Dylan."

My head snapped around and my eyes swiveled to centerstage. There he was, harmonica around his neck, guitar across his body, wearing jeans and a short sleeve shirt. I knew that shirt. Up there he looked enormous.

Although he had already done the solo concert at Town Hall this was a MAJOR deal. Newport was a national event because people came from all over, both performers and audience members. It got reviewed everywhere. This was Bob's first time performing live on a national stage. His manager, Albert Grossman, was a co-founder of the festival. He made sure Bob was going to be in the right spot.

The first song he does is "Talking World War III" from his second album, "The Freewheelin."

He next does "With God On Our Side;" an 11-verse condensation of the essence of American history in war and religion. It was just as powerful as it had been at Town Hall. The last line, "If God's on our side He'll stop the next war," elicited wild applause and people screaming:

"Bobbeeee... Bobbeeee."

(Bob's handwritten lyrics to "God On Our Side")

Next is "Only A Pawn In Their Game" about the murder of Medgar Evers, a black civil rights activist recently killed by a white man. It was a scathing indictment of what was currently happening in the South.

The song following is one that was supposed to be on his second album and would have given him his first national exposure two months earlier. He had been scheduled to do it on the Ed Sullivan show May 12, 1963. It was called "The John Birch Paranoid Talking Blues." The commercial sponsors were not comfortable with Bob performing it. The show's producers told him to do something else. Mr. Sullivan claimed he personally liked the song but:

"My hands are tied."

Bob's reply? He packed up his guitar, walked off the set, then came over to our apartment. He was in a not so pleasant, somewhat mystified, semi-glum mood.

"What's the problem with these corporate people? It's a funny song," he said.

My father sympathized.

"Bobby, there will always be people like that you will run into. You handled it correctly and stood on principle. There will always be bumps along the way. There will be plenty of other opportunities. Isn't your next album being released soon?"

"Yeah, it's supposed to come out in a couple of weeks, but the record company gave me a hard time about that song as well."

"Bobby, you're a smart young man. You'll figure out a way."

"Well, you know, Mac, Albert (Grossman) has arranged for me to perform at the Newport Folk Festival in July."

"You see, opportunities are happening already," Dad replied.

Now here he was on a national stage doing the song.

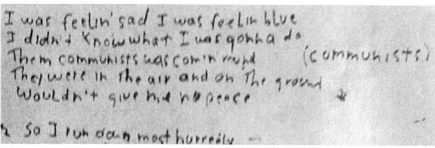

(Bob's handwritten lyrics to "Talking John Birch")

His final scheduled number was "A Hard Rain's-A-Gonna Fall." If anyone in the crowd had not been paying close attention before, they started paying attention then as each line sounded through the air.

It became obvious right then that no matter how talented, famous, or intense any other performer at the festival might be, no one was going to come close to what this crowd was witnessing. Even the Top Dog of all had the integrity and modesty to know that and immediately acknowledge it.

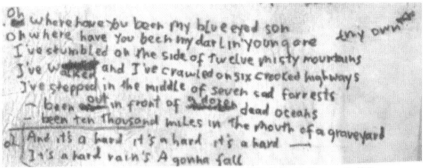

(Bob's handwritten lyrics to "A Hard Rain's A-Gonna Fall")

Bob exited the stage to cries of "More....more.... more." Only an encore would settle down the crowd. He came back out, but not alone. With him were Joan Baez, Peter Paul and Mary, The Freedom Singers and Pete Seeger. They started to form in a semicircle about 10 feet back of the center stage microphone. It looked as if they were going to do a group song. Then something very subtle happened. As they were assembling Pete Seeger said a couple of words in Bob's ear and gave him a slight nudge, like a gentle push forward, so Bob wound up in front of the center microphone by himself, everyone else behind him. None of the cameras filming the event captured it, but that's what happened. Something I never forgot. That nudge was the exact moment Pete

Seeger, The Top Dog, passed the mantle and torch to Bob. As he stood at the microphone with his guitar doing a great rendition of "Blowing In The Wind," the others harmonized in the background.

The song finished to tremendous applause and the group started to sing "We Shall Overcome." It appeared as if Pete wanted Bob to remain out in front, leading the group in that anthem. Even though he had just been elevated front and center above everyone before thousands of people, Bob knew the anthem was bigger than any one man. He backed away from the microphone into the group, guitar slung to his side. Those two numbers... a singular, unforgettable eight-minute piece of history.

That was it for the first night. I went looking for Kevin back where the car had been parked. I found him and Mark and we worked out sleeping arrangements.

Before you knew it, it was Saturday morning. I couldn't wait until 11 am when the workshops started because I was going to find Bob at one of them. Thousands of people were spread out all over the place, sleeping, getting up, or already up.

I saw Kevin. He'd been awake for a while.

"Are you ready, Pete?" he said.

"Ready for what?"

"Something has come up and I have to get back to New York this afternoon."

"You're kidding, right?"

"No, I'm not," he replied.

"When do you have to leave?"

"In about two hours."

I calculated. Two hours would be 10 o'clock. That gave me two hours to find if Bob had arrived early for a workshop and was somewhere on the grounds. I went all over the place searching high and low, but without success. At 10:15 I returned to the car. Everyone got in and the drive back to New York City began. Bob had come a long way since July 1961.

(Bob singing "Blowing in the Wind" – July 26, 1963)

CHAPTER 25:
IT HAPPENED ONE CAMP TIME

In the middle of July 1961, I was getting ready for camp. I knew I would be back home in three weeks, but those were three weeks I wouldn't be around Bob. I tried to make the best of it. Unfortunately, this camp thing didn't turn out to be a particularly good experience for me. There were two popular guys in my age group, one who played the banjo and the other who played the guitar. We did not get along.

When I would say:

"Hey, let's learn from each other and there's a terrific folksinger named Bob Dylan…," they had no interest.

After a week I called my folks.

"Get me out of here," I told my father.

I heard some background chatter which I couldn't quite make out as my father relayed what I was saying to all those who were at the apartment. A distinct voice in the background said:

"Mac, let me speak to him."

Dad handed over the phone and Bob's voice came through the line.

"Just ignore them, Pete. Do your own thing and don't worry about it."

He even wrote me a note to emphasize his point.

"And whatever you do, don't take no back seat that what's his name up there who says you can't sing - Do what you do but do it good and that's the best way you'll beat him or anyone else you want to beat 'take it easy but take it' and you'll win"

– Bob

I decided to grind it out.

Back at 28th St. events were taking some interesting turns...

Before I left I told Bob he could have my bedroom. Kevin had come in and taken over the couch. My mother was now making breakfast for both, and it sometimes got rowdy around the kitchen table in the morning. It was no longer a laissez-faire attitude like when I was there. Before, when Bob had written things at night, they would be put away in the living room drawer by my mother the next morning and we'd wait till he was ready to share it. That was not the routine with Kevin. If they hadn't spent time together the night before...

"So, what happened last night, Bobby? Write anything new?

Let's see it. Let's hear it," Kevin would say.

Many times, Bob would mumble and continue to eat his eggs, or oatmeal. Sometimes, when he wasn't in the mood, he would do more than mumble. Not exactly an argument, but:

"Play nice and eat your breakfast," my mother would admonish them.

While this household arrangement lasted only for the three weeks I was at camp, something momentous began a week and a half after I was gone and concluded after I got back.

Since the beginning the full story how Robert Shelton, national music critic for the New York Times, and writer of the Dylan biography, "No Direction Home," got on the early Dylan band wagon has not been correctly documented. I saw it as it happened.

The review Robert Shelton wrote about Bob that appeared in the September 29, 1961 edition of the New York Times, for all intents and purposes, launched Bob's career. The historical significance of that review cannot be overstated. Of course, it was Bob himself who sold his talents when Shelton came down to Gerde's to see him and the headlining act, The Greenbriar Boys, on September 26.

Kevin understood advertising and promotion just like Bob was a natural writer and poet. The first thing a promoter thinks of is how to get more people into the audience. Kevin had watched Bob's development for a year and knew it was time for a step up. While pushing Bob AFTER he made the big step forward was not on his agenda, helping him get to that stage was.

In 1961 where did people get their information from?... Newspapers. Who in newspapers would be the most advantageous for Bob?... Entertainment people. Who among them would be best to get in his corner?... Those who did reviews of performers and records. What was the most influential newspaper?... The New

York Times. Who was the most influential reviewer?... After doing his homework Kevin determined it was Robert Shelton. So, the task was how a Mr. Nobody, Kevin Krown, could get Robert Shelton to take notice of a second Mr. Nobody, Bob Dylan?

One thing no one could accuse Kevin of was not having chutzpah. He was a born salesman, with a tongue so sharp and smooth he could put things in a way that the thread of the story was so believable you'd be compelled to hear it out until the end. Things would seem (key word "seem") put together so logically that you might think it all possibly could be true. Now if you REALLY gave him something to work with... say a 20-year-old Bob Dylan... you fill in the rest.

The first thing that started were the phone calls. Kevin would call Mr. Shelton at work.

"Hello. My name is Kevin Krown and there is a new performer Mr. Shelton should be made aware of. His name is Bob Dylan. Is he in?"

"I'm sorry, Mr. Shelton is not available," was always the answer.

I say "always" because it wasn't just one call a day. It was a barrage of phone calls every day.

It is true that on July 29, 1961, Robert Shelton had been sent by the New York Times to see the Riverside Church hootenanny broadcast in New York City. That was just after Kevin had begun his phone campaign, but had not yet gotten through, personally, to Mr. Shelton. Even though Mr. Shelton mentioned Bob's name in his review of the concert, Bob was just one of many there and Mr. Shelton was a very busy man.

Next, Kevin found out where Mr. Shelton lived. Not only was Mr. Shelton getting several phone calls each day, he was now getting telegrams at his home. Finally, one day Kevin called the office and was put on hold. There was a click and then:

"This is Robert Shelton."

I've always believed Mr. Shelton picked up that time because he wanted to get rid of that pest, Krown, with the intent of telling him:

"Okay, pal, I took your call. You made your pitch. I have your number. I'll get back to you first chance I get," – then lose the number.

But, just like no one had ever met anyone like Bob, Mr. Shelton had never run into anyone like Kevin... and Kevin was selling Bob. Once Mr. Shelton picked up the phone to talk to Kevin, he was a goner. By the time Kevin got through with the first conversation you would have thought he was talking about the King of Valhalla. Mr. Shelton was intrigued. They had some more conversations and Kevin mentioned several names of people Bob had befriended. They were names Mr. Shelton knew and could reach out to learn more about who Bob Dylan was.

I can't make the claim there weren't other external factors at work that led to Bob and Mr. Shelton interacting. I only can tell you what I witnessed. And what I witnessed sure didn't hurt.

"I've done my job, Bobby," said Kevin. "Now it's time to do yours."

CHAPTER 26: OVER JULY

When I got back from camp at the beginning of August Kevin had to give up his sleeping spot. He still came into the city each day to finish up the Shelton business. I was going to tell Bob it was okay for him to stay in my room, and I would take the couch, at least until school started.

"Certainly not," said my mother. "The school year starts in less than a month and that is not the way for you to get proper rest until then."

Though he couldn't know it at the time, that encouraging note Bob wrote me just a couple of weeks earlier had a very direct developmental impact on me going forward.

In the Summer of 1963, after Kevin and I returned from Newport, my father and I went down to Washington Square park - me with my guitar and my father with a couple of harmonicas. When we arrived that day, I spotted one of the two musician guys that had been so dismissive of me at camp in 1961. I was very relaxed as I walked over to him.

"Hey, man, how you doing?" I said like nothing had ever happened. "I see you're playing the guitar now, not just the banjo."

"Yeah," he replied. "V---- and me got together after camp and he gave me some lessons."

"That's nice. How's he doing these days?"

"I don't know," he answered. "We kind of lost touch."

"Mind if we play a couple of those old tunes you played at camp?" I said.

I unpacked my guitar and we started flat picking. He was trying to keep up.

"How'd you get so good?" he exclaimed.

"Well, you know the fellow I told you about who was staying with my folks while we were at camp?"

"Not really," he answered.

"He was nice enough to show me a few things. You may have heard of him by now."

"What's his name?" he asked.

"Bob Dylan."

He looked, for a moment, as if someone knocked all the air out of him.

"Yeah," I said. "Really cool guy. Matter of fact he came over to our apartment right after his recent Town Hall concert."

"You were there? I was there, too," he said, his eyes wide.

"Yes. It was also to congratulate me on my being accepted to Harvard."

Technically, that wasn't the case since I didn't get the notification until April 15, not April 14 when Bob came by. Bob did congratulate me a few days later, though.

"Anyway, it was nice seeing you again. Got to go. Good luck," I finished.

Bang! Deal done! Game over! How right the advice Bob had given me in those few lines.

But, let's not get too far ahead...

A week after I returned from camp my mother was washing the dishes and Bob came into the kitchen. She turned her head.

"Eve, there's a song I'm reworking, and I'd like your opinion. I've sung it before, but not this way. You're the first to hear it."

She shut off the water, so it was quiet. Her back was still to him as she began drying the dishes. Bob sat in the rocking chair and began to play. He often liked to sit in the rocking chair when doing new stuff. It relaxed him. He could rock back and forth, or not, depending on his mood. As soon as he started to play Mom stopped her drying. She wanted to hear the words and didn't want to disturb anything about the moment. Her back remained turned and she didn't move the entire time until he was done.

"So, Eve, what do you think?"

She turned around.

"That was magnificent, did you write that?"

"Nah," he said. "I kind of picked it up. I was thinking of doing it like that."

"It's very powerful. What's it called?"

"'House of the Rising Sun.'"

"It's a wonderful piece."

"Yeah, I picked it up from Dave Van Ronk."

"Oh," she exclaimed. "Did he write it?"

"Nah. But I really like the way he does it. I was thinking of doing it like that."

"Well, you should give Dave credit when you do it on stage. It would be a big compliment to him and he's such a nice man."

"Ok," he said.

The same issue came up again when Bob was to record his first album. He knew that Dave intended to record it later, on his own record. It was Dave's signature number, and he was going to use it to put in that extra oomph factor. The thing was, by then, it had become a crowd favorite with Bob's live audiences. He thought Dave might be angry if he recorded it first. He wrestled with it. In the end "House of the Rising Sun" was included on Bob's first album. Dave was upset when it happened - for a short while. He got over it and the two remained friends.

CHAPTER 27:
TWO IDES IN AUGUST AND ONE IN SEPTEMBER

The last week in August was hot. Everything was moving along like a well-oiled machine. Robert Shelton was paying attention to Bob. Suze Rotolo was now in the picture. Bob had met her on July 29 at the Riverside Church concert. When he got up the morning after that concert my mother and Kevin listened to him gushing about this girl who he said was unlike anyone he'd ever met. Mike Porco had committed to a second paying engagement for Bob at Gerde's at the end of September.

In that last week, Bob announced he'd been offered $20 to sing at an event.

"That's wonderful," my parents said. "What's the occasion?"

"It's some Socialist function," Bob replied.

For a moment there was silence. The concern on my mother's face... My father, calm as always when the situation required a level head, was pragmatic.

"Why would you want to perform at a Socialist function?" he asked.

"Yes, why?" Mom echoed my father's words.

It was a moment one of the most significant political history lessons took place in the McKenzie household. Bob picked up on the seriousness of their concerns.

"Why not?" he asked.

"Bobby, do you understand the possible implications and ramifications if you sing at an event like this?" my mother replied.

My parents knew how easy it was to have a label stamped on someone, justified or not, and once that happened how that label could follow them around like a mill stone no matter how smart they, or their intentions were. My father gave Bob a more detailed, thorough talk than he'd ever done before - from personal experience. He used the National Maritime Union, the McCarthy era with its bogus Communist scare as the main tools. And yes, Paul Robeson. He wanted nothing but the greatest success for Bob. He really cared about him.

"But, Pete Seeger," Bob started to say.

"You're not Pete Seeger, Bobby," my mother interjected. "He has a different point of view. You're a different type of artist and you must be free to do what you want without being dictated to by any group, pigeonholed, or labeled by anyone."

Some of his contemporaries were trying to reel Bob into their faction. The question was straightforward and non-judgmental.

"Is it the money that makes you want to do it, or 'The Cause'?"

For another young person to get hurt for the wrong reasons was pointless. They'd both seen too many people get robbed of their rightful place, and their character assassinated, simply because they "happened to be there." Why naively give ammunition to be used against them later?

The question was repeated.

"Is it the money or 'The Cause'?"

Whatever decision he came to they would respect his judgement. It was a concern from the heart, and experience,

Bob didn't do the performance. It was his own choice.

Soon after, he was sitting in the living room with Kevin. They were talking though I couldn't hear the words.

The first time Bob was booked for his first paying gig at Gerde's in April, my mother had called up everybody she knew to tell them about this incredible young talent they should go see. I'd told all my friends at the time, but they were underage.

Mom came into the room and the talking stopped.

Out of the blue Bob says:

"Eve, why don't you become my manager?"

She looked at him and smiled.

"Bobby," she said, "thank you for the compliment. Although I've met many people in the entertainment business, knowing them and managing someone are two completely different things. I'm not cut out for that. I really wouldn't know what to do. And, as you know, I have other responsibilities," looking over at me. "It's a full-time job. You're a very special talent and you need someone who has been doing it a long time, knows all the ins and outs, agents, contacts, contracts and so much more. It's a lovely thought you should ask, but I'm not equipped to do it. Someone who'll be right for you will come along sooner than you think."

Bob understood instantly. That was a great thing about him. You didn't have to repeat things. He got it the first time.

When September started Bob came home at dusk.

"I'm going to be playing harmonica on several tracks of Carolyn Hester's next album," he stated.

Carolyn was Richard Farina's wife at the time. She was originally from Texas and Bob, you remember, first met her and Richard on his trip to Cambridge, Massachusetts earlier in the summer. This was a different situation than Belafonte because Bob, Carolyn and Richard had become friends and understood how each other worked. He was very enthused to show what he could do in the proper setting.

A week after that he was downtown in a loft with Carolyn and

Richard rehearsing the songs he was going to play on. They were also swapping guitar tunes. As it would happen, Carolyn's record producer, John Hammond, stopped by to see how things were going. That was his first contact with Bob.

Bob came back to 28th St. right after the rehearsal.

"I had a really good time with Carolyn and Richard. Their producer, John Hammond, came by. Carolyn introduced us. He hung about for a while. Right before he left he told me:

"Come by and see me. I think you have something."

His spirit level was elevated. He knew how important John Hammond was.

"Don't tell anyone," he said.

CHAPTER 28:

BROTHERHOOD OF THE TRAVELING PANTS

September 26, 1961 was a big day for Bob. It was opening night for his second paying gig at Gerde's Folk City and Robert Shelton was going to be in the audience to write a review of the whole evening. He was opening for a group called the Greenbriar Boys. They were the headliners and a well-known bluegrass band. Bob had previously brought John Herald, their guitar player, up to visit my parents. He was very friendly and could play the country style guitar like it was a natural extension of his arm.

Even though Bob had recently moved out he had come over to the apartment the day before to say "Hello" and get ready for the big night. While he was a little antsy, he was still very together in those situations, or certainly gave the outward appearance of it. He wanted to look nice in his "Bob Dylan" way. Standing in front of our big hallway mirror he kept adjusting his cap to see which angle looked best. It looked good on him no matter how it was placed. He had on a nice vest and was trying to decide whether he should wear it. His shirt was light colored. His boots were in the kitchen waiting to be put on. He was in his socks and underwear. The sound of a sewing machine was whirring away. In the reflection in the mirror, he could see my mother at the kitchen table running material under the automatic needle.

Bob felt he didn't have the proper pair of pants for the opening, so he decided to come to tailor, Eve. His waist size and my father's were about the same. Dad had longer legs. My mother had gone into the closet and gotten a nice pair of freshly pressed khakis.

"Try these on, Bobby."

"Okay," he says.

He takes off his boots and jeans and puts on the pants in the living room. The cap and vest are not on yet.

"Now put your boots back on," says my mother.

"Okay," he says, again.

"Good," says Mom. "Now let's go into the kitchen."

They go into the kitchen.

"Now adjust the pants around your waist to where they're most comfortable."

He adjusts them.

"They fit pretty good," he says.

"Do you have a belt?" she asks.

"Yeah, on my old pants."

"Peter, get Bobby his belt."

I get the belt from the jeans he had taken off and bring it to him.

"Now adjust it to the tightness you're going to when you wear them," she tells him.

He does, wiggling a little to get it just right.

"They look good on you," she says.

She looks down at the bottom of the trousers that are touching his boots.

"Aside from the length, they fit nicely."

"Yeah, they're a bit long," he agrees.

"Now stand still. I'm going to pin them up a little to make them shorter, so they just break on your boots."

My mother pins up both hems.

Bob moves around a little bit.

"Feels right," he says.

"Good," says Mom. "Now take them off so I can finish them."

He sits in the rocking chair, takes off his boots and places them next to it. He stands up, takes off his pants and hands them to Mom. He comes back into the living room and sits down next to me in his skivvies. Both of us start listening to the sewing machine in the kitchen stitching away. Then, I remember the different shaped guitar case he came in with sitting in a corner.

"What's that?" I ask him.

"Oh, it's another guitar I got. It's sounds different than the last one."

In a flash I open the case and take it out. It has an all-natural finish with a repair near the bridge and a different tone than his Martin 00-17. It was a Gibson J-50.

Bob was very particular about his guitar strings. They were always "Black Diamond" flat wound steel strings. On the 00-17 Martin he used medium gauge because it was smaller than the J-50 and couldn't tolerate more tension. On the larger bodied J-50 he used heavy gauge. I immediately noticed the difference in feel. It took a little more force to press the strings down.

Bob gets up, puts on the vest, picks up his cap and goes to the mirror to adjust it.

The sewing stops.

"Come into the kitchen," my mother says.

He goes back into the kitchen. My mother gives him the pants. He puts them back on... then his boots. He buckles the belt.

"Hey", he exclaims, "they're just right."

He goes back in the hallway, looks into the mirror, adjusts his cap again, looks himself up-and-down, then looks at Mom.

"Everything's just right," he says to her.

When he comes back into the living room and takes the khakis off he notices the label on them.

"Hey, Eve, it says Brooks Brothers."

"Yes, Bobby, only the best for you."

"Wow," he says, pulling up his old pair of jeans.

Thirty hours later Bob Dylan stepped onto the Gerde's stage wearing an almost perfectly fitting pair of Brooks Brothers khakis. Three days later the review of his performance that night appeared in the New York Times.

****

(NY Times Review -September 29, 1961)
20-Year-Old Singer Is Bright New Face at Gerde's Club
By ROBERT SHELTON

A bright new face in folk music is appearing at Gerde's Folk City. Although only 20 years old, Bob Dylan is one of the most distinctive stylists to play a Manhattan cabaret in months.

Resembling a cross between a choir boy and a beatnik, Mr. Dylan has a cherubic look and a mop of tousled hair he partly covers with a Huck Finn black corduroy cap. His clothes may need a bit of tailoring, but when he works his guitar, harmonica or piano and composes new songs faster than he can remember them, there is no doubt that he is bursting at the seams with talent.

Mr. Dylan's voice is anything but pretty. He is consciously trying to recapture the rude beauty of a Southern field hand musing in melody on his porch. All the "husk and bark" are left on his notes and a searing intensity pervades his songs.

Slow-Motion Mood.

Mr. Dylan is both comedian and tragedian. Like a vaudeville actor on the rural circuit, he offers a variety of droll musical monologues: "Talking Bear Mountain" lampoons the overcrowding of an excursion boat, "Talking New York" satirizes his troubles in gaining recognition and "Talking Havah Nagilah" burlesques the folk-music craze and the singer himself.

In his serious vein, Mr. Dylan seems to be performing in a slow-motion film. Elasticized phrases are drawn out until you think they may snap. He rocks his head and body, closes his eyes in reverie and seems to be groping for a word or a mood, then resolves the tension benevolently by finding the word and the mood.

He may mumble the text of "House of the Rising Sun" in a scarcely understandable growl or sob, or clearly enunciate the poetic poignancy of a Blind Lemon Jefferson blues: "One kind favor I ask of you--See that my grave is kept clean."

Mr. Dylan's highly personalized approach toward folk song is still evolving. He has been sopping up influences like a sponge. At times, the drama he aims at is off-target melodrama and his stylization threatens to topple over as a mannered excess. But if not for every taste, his music-making has the mark of originality and inspiration, all the more noteworthy for his youth. Mr. Dylan is vague about his antecedents and birthplace, but it matters less where he has been than where he is going, and that would seem to be straight up.

****

Everything had come together. Bob's career was at the next level.

Months later he calls her.

Eve," he says, "I met this man, Albert Grossman. He wants to manage me. Should I sign?"

Over the summer Kevin had been checking various management entities. Albert Grossman's name was high on the list. He had discussed a lot of his findings with my folks. My mother was familiar with who Grossman was. He handled Odetta, Judy Collins, and was working on something with Bob's friends, Peter Yarrow and Paul Stookey, and a singer, Mary Travers. When it was finalized they would become the group, Peter, Paul and Mary.

She tells him:

"You have a rave review from Robert Shelton that's given you a big boost. The wave generated by it won't last forever... That's the nature of show business. You need to take advantage of the wave while it's there. It's a great opportunity. If he wants you take him."

No claim is being made that it is that phone call alone that made Bob decide to take Albert as his manager. It was a big decision for him, and he didn't want to make a mistake. I don't know who else he might've asked about it. All I know is he asked someone he trusted, and she said, "Yes."

Thirty years later, in the last phone call my mother had with Bob before she died, the review came up again. She was sitting on the living room couch and Bob was at his home in California. It was three weeks after the conversation I had with his lawyer about selling his early lyrics. I was sitting next to her and could hear both sides of the conversation. She mentioned Kevin. Bob's reply was unexpected.

"Kevin? Kevin who?"

"Kevin Krown," she said.

"Who is Kevin Krown? I don't know anyone with that name," said the voice at the other end of the line.

The look on my mother's face was one of dismay. She looked at me. I didn't say a word. The next thing he said was:

"Eve, must I thank everyone who helped me along the way?"

Suddenly, the expression on my mother's face changed and the tone of her voice became that of one scolding an unruly teen.

"Yes, you must thank everyone that helped you along the way."

Hanging up the phone, my mother looked over at me as I shook my head, silently.

-From the William Pagel archives-

(Bob on opening night wearing Brooks Brothers pants)

CHAPTER 29:
ROLL ON COLUMBIA
THROUGH THE HURRICANE

On September 30th, 1961, Bob went into the recording studio with Carolyn Hester. The review by Robert Shelton had appeared the day before. If Mr. Hammond was having any second thoughts about meeting with Bob individually, the article had to erase any doubt about his first gut instinct toward him.

A lot of people who were not there seem to have their own version leading to the Hammond/Dylan connection. The only thing that really matters is that on October 26, 1961, Bob Dylan put his signature on a Columbia recording contract.

On the heels of the initial buzz from the review Izzy Young decided to arrange a solo concert for Bob on November 4, 1961, at Carnegie Chapter Hall. Remember, Jack Elliott had given his own concert there nine months earlier. My parents, Kevin, Duke, Millie and I were there. There was a small, raised stage, but Bob had decided to stand in front of it on the flat floor, a microphone in front of him. He knew a lot of the people attending, so he was more relaxed than otherwise. Being at the same level footing as the audience made it more intimate. The folding chairs were set so there was a center aisle 3 feet wide with seating on either side. Before starting his set he decided to tell a funny story about what happened on his way there. As an introduction to his 15th song, "Talking Merchant Marine," he looked over at my father and Duke and said, "Got some seamen in the house tonight."

My mother squeezed my father's arm.

His remark emboldened me and a couple of songs later I said in a slightly raised voice, "Do Hard Travelin'."

He smiled and looked my way, but didn't do it. He had a specific list he didn't want to deviate from.

After the concert he came over to me and said, "No big deal. I can do it for you anytime back at the apartment."

Most accounts refer to him performing 22 songs; it was 23.

While he really didn't have to do a concert at that specific time there was a reason for it. He agreed with Kevin and Izzy. Since he was going to record his first album soon it was a good opportunity to get a sense for what material might go over best, as well as what material he felt most comfortable doing.

I've always been bothered by comments made about how nervous Bob seemed and that with only 53 people in attendance the place was almost empty. If Jack Elliott were asked, the first thing he would tell you is there are traditionally about 100 seats in the venue to begin with. However you cut it the place was more than half full.

I didn't see Bob's recording session with Carolyn Hester, or the sessions of his debut album, but eventually I did attend one. At the end of July 1975 Bob was recording a new album for his label, Columbia, in New York City. I was managing a recording studio in the Village and Doug Pomeroy, an in-house engineer at Columbia who had all access, asked me if I wanted to come and watch...

I was going out with a very pretty woman at the time so I knew any security personnel wouldn't question my attendance. It's just the way things were at that time.

Doug takes us to the Columbia Studios on 52nd St. Security lets the three of us right through. We get up to one of the recording areas. It's not the big one. It's smaller. We go into the control room. The recording engineer looks up, sees Doug and the girl I am with and gives a thumbs up. Bob isn't there. He's in the recording room itself finishing a song. You can hear it through the control room speakers. As soon as he is done he walks through the door to the control room and sits down in a chair 25 feet away, opposite us. The lights are dim. He's casually dressed in a white shirt that hangs outside his jeans. He appears very serious and begins talking with his producer, Don DeVito, seated next to him. The musicians remain in the recording room. The drummer is relaxing over at the piano playing a ragtime tune to keep loose. I had heard a woman's voice on the last track and can see through the soundproof glass separating the control room from the recording room. It is Emmylou Harris. Seeing her reminded me of Gram Parsons when he was a freshman at Harvard. We briefly knew each other and jammed a couple of times. He and Emmylou were close before he died in 1973 at 26.

I remain in my spot until Bob is through talking with Mr. DeVito and is sitting alone in the chair looking over some notes. No one else is talking to him and it is obvious no one will until he gives a signal it's okay. He doesn't know we are there. After waiting a little bit, I walk across the control room.

"Hi, Bob."

He looks up and it's the same look on his face as Woodstock seven years earlier when Hooper and I showed up at his house.

He could have snapped at me for interrupting him, but doesn't.

"Oh, hey, Pete."

Before he has a chance to say anything else, I tell him:

"I brought my girlfriend with me."

He looks across the room. I don't know if he could see her, but that doesn't matter.

"How are you?" he asks.

"I'm fine. Mom and Dad are fine as well. They send their love. I see you're working, though, and don't want to disturb you. It sounds great. I was told you were here. Hope you don't mind?"

"Nah."

"Terrific. I'll leave you alone so you can get back to work."

I give him a goodbye sign and go back across the room.

"You saw his grin," I tell her.

Bob finishes looking at the pieces of paper he is holding and walks into the recording room. The door is closed behind him. He sits down in a chair in the middle, picks up a guitar, strums a few chords, then starts to play the opening of a song. Everyone in the room scrambles from where they are to get to their spots. The first drumbeat is right on time, as is the bass. There is no count off like most artists - one, two, three, four and then the first chord. Sometimes, it just begins when he gets that Bob feeling.

They go through a whole song. It is also the only time I ever heard it. It doesn't appear on the released album, and I can't remember the lyrics because my focus was split in two directions. While I was trying to register the song there was this other guitar player sitting a little ways off from Bob, to his right. It appeared as if he was supposed to be playing second acoustic guitar. There was a separate microphone for him. I say appeared because he had no idea how to play the guitar. He was just playing random notes. There must have been a reason he was there, but I could never figure it out. He didn't know any of the chords to the song, aimlessly plucking away during the take. It was one of the oddest things I've ever seen in a studio. Fortunately, his guitar playing doesn't appear anywhere on the final album. Maybe his microphone had never been turned on.

When the number finishes the musicians start to move from

their places anticipating a tape playback, but Bob decides to go into the next song. They rush back to their spots. While a different take than this one was used on the album it was a long song, like a giant tsunami right from the beginning to the end; the odd guitar player still plucking away.

Bob appeared to have blocked out every other sound and distraction. The concentration and intensity was unwavering. You could have dropped a hand grenade in the room and it wouldn't have phased him. The rendition was a mission. His guitar playing was automatic. The voice, body, harmonica and guitar were just different parts of one completely integrated instrument. His attitude was infectious. There was now this very small group of people pumping out something as if they were one. It is rare to see the gelling of a song so quickly in a session. Everyone in the control room could see it unfolding tighter and tighter as the song got longer and longer. I feel privileged to have seen it with my own eyes and I've seen many special Bob performances. The end came. The spell hung in the air for a few moments when the word, "Playback?" came from the control room. Bob nodded, put down his guitar and moved to another stool.

Playback of "The Hurricane" began.

This time some of the musicians came into the control room. Bob remained sitting in the recording room listening. Every now and then he put his hands up to his head and fluffed up his hair; an old habit. When the playback ended he didn't say anything. The control room voice came over the speakers:

" Nice take, Bob."

He looked up, but I couldn't see the expression on his face. He sat there a couple more minutes, nodded to Scarlet Rivera, the violin player and said something to Emmylou Harris.

If you've ever been in a recording studio time speeds up. What you think was twenty minutes suddenly becomes an hour. The musicians who had come into the control room during playback started shuffling back into the recording room getting ready for the next take. Bob was looking over another piece of paper. As the recording room door closed and the studio was soundproof once again, another person entered the control room from the hallway, a small entourage in tow. It was the actor, Jerry Orbach, pre - "Law and Order" days.

"Geez, how many people does Bob know?" I said out loud."

That thought brought up a memory of a decade earlier when Bob was visiting 28th St. and talking about fame. He was lighthearted about it.

"You know, you know when I knew I had arrived? When Albert (Grossman) said to me, 'Which actress or model do you want to go out with. I'll just make a call and it's done.'"

"Some things in this world never change," my father replied with a knowing look.

I knew the recording session could go all night and the control room was beginning to get crowded. We made a quiet exit, went down in the elevator and walked out into the night.

CHAPTER 30: THE AFTERMATH

The next afternoon following Bob's recording session I was at my art studio on 21st St. The phone rings. It's my mother.

"Hi, mom."

"Bob wants to see you."

"What do you mean?"

"He just came to the apartment and wants to see you."

It was like the call 14 years earlier on February 16, 1961, when she wanted me to come down to Gerde's after Jack Elliott's concert.

I was out the door before the phone was hung up. It's normally a 15-minute walk from the studio to the apartment. I made it in half the time. I turned the corner on Fifth Avenue and 28th St. and approached our street door. Even though it was a Thursday the street was relatively empty save for an enormous red Cadillac convertible parked right in front of it. Yep, Bob was in the building. I sped up the stairs and opened the apartment door. The living room was empty except for a hat with a feather sticking up in the middle of the living room couch. I picked up the hat and tried it on. It was heavy. I took it off and put it back exactly where I found it. Bob is wearing that same hat on the cover of "Desire," the album he was currently recording.

I go into the kitchen. Everyone is there; my father, my mother, Bob and a young woman accompanying him, all sitting around the kitchen table

"Hi, Bob," I say as I sit down in the vacant rocking chair.

"Hi, Pete," he says and introduces his friend to me.

I look at him. He's wearing jeans, a white shirt and brown leather jacket. The light is much brighter than at the recording studio. I can see every line on his face, that is if there were any. He is clean-shaven and his hair instead of being somewhat curly seems to be straight, hanging over his forehead. Probably pressed down from his hat. It's dark brown. He almost looks like a fifth Beatle.

"So, what is it you're up to these days?" he asks.

I tell him about managing the downtown recording studio.

"That sounds terrific, Pete."

Suddenly, I go into overdrive. Adrenaline has that effect.

"You should hear this new song Bob wrote that we heard last night. It's amazing. It's about this boxer who was framed for murder, and he describes and exposes how it's a lie verse after verse after verse."

I had heard of the Hurricane Carter case before, though I didn't know all the details.

"When you listen to it you have to know he's innocent. I should get the guitar and let Bob sing some of it for you"

My father steps in.

"I know you're excited to see Bobby again, but he probably has a long day ahead."

"But it's such a great song, you should hear it."

I look over at Bob and he has a Mona Lisa smile. I was relieved to see that instead of a look of annoyance. He didn't sing it, but went over some of the lyrics.

There were a lot of questions I wanted to ask him, but the conversation reverted to a topic that was being discussed before I got there. It concerned the audio tapes he'd made at our apartment from 1961 to 1963. They were stored in a special cabinet in the living room. Before I arrived, my parents had mentioned to Bob something I'd told them in passing a few days earlier. They all wanted clarification, so I began to explain...

"Bob, someone I've been working with at the recording studio is well connected in the music business. He knows about our relationship and the tapes. He wants to buy them for $90,000."

"What's he going to do with them?" he asks.

I knew by the tone of his voice what he was thinking.

"Maybe he wants to make a record from them."

"Yeah," he says. "People are making bootlegs of stuff I do, like concerts, all the time. There seems to be a network out there for that."

Now, like Bob's handwritten lyrics I would discuss with his lawyer 16 years later, the tapes could have been sold without asking, or telling him about it. Technically, my parents had purchased the blank tapes and they owned the tape recorder. Physically, it was their property. They could be sold to a third-party with no questions asked. It would be perfectly legal. But, as always, my parents felt they had an ethical responsibility to let Bob know and get his feelings about it first.

"That's a lot of money," he says.

This was 1975. That amount handled properly, and with inflation, could easily be worth over $1 million in today's terms. It was serious money, or a couple of houses.

Since I had listened to the recordings more than my parents, I began describing them. I went over each one telling him how good he sounded. As I went along my folks would add comments of things they remembered. I started with the 1961 Thanksgiving tape (more on that later). One thing that tickled him was when I repeated what he said to me that night."

"Here's a good song for you, Peter," as he started to sing "Baby Let Me Follow You Down."

It may have been a good song, but I was clueless back then what it was truly about. He never knew that and laughed.

I talked about "Riding Number Nine" (the correct title is 'Lonesome Whistle Blues'), and my (overly)enthusiastic behavior during his 1963 Town Hall concert. After thinking for a moment, he says:

"Oh, yeah, I remember that."

Then came the discussion of possibly doing a deal.

Bob says:

"It's fine with me, but there might be an issue. I wish we had talked about this a while ago. It would have been easy. Of course, I'd have given the go-ahead, but here's the situation now. As you know, I left Columbia and signed with Asylum records. Then I left Asylum and re-signed with Columbia. That's the problem. There was a period, for a few months, when I didn't have a record company contract. You could've done anything you wanted. But now that I've resigned with Columbia, they're the ones that make the legal decisions. I'm happy to say 'Yes,' but the legal ramifications I can't control. The executives at Columbia might not be happy with it. Somewhere down the road they'll find out and might go after whoever bought and started distributing them. It could become a very messy and expensive legal hassle. They might ask if I knew anything about it. If I say "yes" the record company could decide to sue me."

My father says:

"Bobby, we completely understand what you are saying. Even if the person interested in the purchase is not concerned about any legal issues, or the cost of possible litigation down the line, it would not be right to put yourself in a potential compromising position where you might have to lie to protect yourself."

In the quiet moment that followed I processed my father's

remark. It took only an instant for me to think what would be the big issue if Bob said:

"I didn't know. Don't blame me..."

But, my folks would know.

Bob sensed my dilemma.

"Pete, don't worry about it. There'll be lots of other opportunities."

It was the same thing my parents said to him about the Ed Sullivan incident over a decade earlier.

While his comment seemed to make sense, I was no longer that 15-year-old kid. I had a few angles of my own and wasn't convinced about the legal logic. Then, my second wind of reason took over. The tapes, in fact, belonged to my parents and they had the right to make whatever decision they thought appropriate. What would have been wrong is if I had taken the tapes and done the deal anyway. I could have pulled it off. I knew Bob well enough to know he might be pissed, but he would never say a word. That, however, meant going against every principle my parents stood for. It was those core beliefs that made Bob trust, love and respect them in the first place; and helped form me.

As he left, I said:

"That's a cool set of wheels you have outside."

What I really wanted to say but didn't:

"Hey, a Cadillac. Pretty good car to drive... after a war."

For those who don't know Dylanspeak, listen to the seventh verse of "Talking World War III Blues" on 'The Freewheelin,' his second album. You'll get it.

He was walking down the stairs with his friend, waving back up with his left hand holding that heavy hat in his right.

(Hat that Bob wore to the apartment)

CHAPTER 31:
TWO YEARS BEFORE THE MAST

An unannounced visit happened the same way two years earlier in 1973 with another buzz on the downstairs 28th St. street door. It was 12 years since Bob first walked up our apartment stairs, guitar and suitcase in hand. The days when all the building street level doors were open had gone. To get into the building now you had to be buzzed in. My mother went to the apartment door and talked into the intercom.

"Yes, who is it?"

"It's Me, Eve."

"Oh... Come on up. Glad you're home."

She pushed the door-open buzzer button.

He was in good shape because he was almost up all the stairs by the time she took her finger off it and not even out of breath. Tucked under his arm was a copy of his book "Writings and Drawings." It had just come out.

He took the book from under his arm and said:

"I want to give you this."

"You don't have to do that, Bobby. Seeing you is enough."

I was watching. He hadn't expected me there and this was really their moment.

He goes into the kitchen and sits at the kitchen table. He opens the book to the front page and starts writing. He finishes and hands it to my mother. She looks at it. Her eyes tear up and she gives him a kiss.

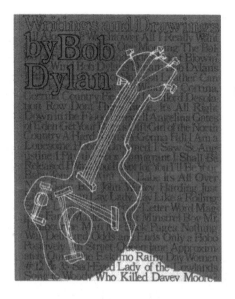

For Eve & Mac, who were there when it Began, Thanks for Everything, love, Bob

"How's Mac?" he asks.

"He's out in California right now. Duke and Millie wanted him to come out and visit them. Millie volunteered to drive him from there to Virginia City. He hasn't been back there since he left 50 years ago. It's very sweet of them."

"They're good people," he says.

"Yes, they are," she answers.

Bob was very proud of the book. He pointed to his drawings in it. He had come a long way from his earlier sketches in 1961 at our apartment. He was more excited about the artwork than the printing of the lyrics.

His curiosity turned to how I was doing.

"You know, Pete, I'm building a house in Malibu, California. What's happening in the architecture department?"

He knew, at last count, I had planned to make architecture my profession and should have been going great guns at it. He knew I had remained in Cambridge after graduating college to attend the prestigious Harvard Graduate School of Design and become an architect. Was Bob hinting what I thought he was? With him looking intently at me my first words were:

"I was completely at odds with the faculty."

I could see by his look an explanation was in order, so I gave him one. I told him that my vision and the school's about the meaning and purpose of architecture were like oil and water and went through a litany of design theories to clarify things as much as possible.

"I know I'm being very technical, but it's the only way I know how to express it," I finished up. "I felt like I was in a 'straight-jacket.' My brain couldn't justify two more years of their torture, so I left."

I was a bit nervous telling him. I looked at him. I couldn't tell if he understood, or if it was a hint of sadness in his eye. He turned to my mother and said:

"What type of elementary school did you send Pete to? He came out alright."

Knowing Bob's penchant for timing I would like to think while he was seeking advice on his children's education, by changing the subject at that moment, he was also reassuring me the choice I made regarding leaving architecture was ok.

"Bobby," Mom replied, "look how you came out. You came out just fine. You're perfectly capable of handling those decisions yourself."

She was reassuring HIM.

The topic switched to movies.

Bob had been involved with a film a couple years earlier called "Pat Garrett and Billy the Kid." He wrote the score and songs for it. It starred James Coburn as Pat Garrett, Kris Kristofferson as Billy the Kid, and a group of several veteran Hollywood characters. Bob also had a part as an actor. He was always interested in the film process. Many don't know that in the early 60's, after "The Freewheelin" was released, serious discussions with J.D. Salinger's representatives about making the book, "The Catcher in The Rye," into a movie took place.

Bob told us back then:

"Albert (Grossman) has been talking with some people in Hollywood. They want me to play Holden Caulfield in a film version of 'The Catcher in The Rye.'"

"The Catcher in The Rye" was a book Bob and I had talked about while he was living with us. It was a must read for all the "intellectual" in-crowd during my high school sophomore year. My parents had an original hardcover edition. I liked it, but there were some angles that didn't register with me the first time around. A few days before Bob left for his first trip to Cambridge I was going out the door and said to him:

"I read this book everyone's all hot about. It's called "The Catcher in The Rye" by someone named J.D. Salinger. You should read it and let me know what you think. There's a copy right over there in the bookcase."

I didn't think any more about it until my mother brought up the subject the day after Bob left for Cambridge.

"Peter," she said, "there's a surprise for you. In all the confusion as Bobby was leaving for Cambridge when Duke and Millie came by I forgot."

"What is it?" I asked.

"You know the book you mentioned to Bobby last week that all your friends are reading?"

"What about it?"

"Why don't you go over to the bookcase in the living room," she said.

I couldn't imagine why going and getting the book from the shelf was any kind of surprise, but I went out to the living room and pulled it out. I went back into the kitchen and put it on the table.

"Open it," she told me.

"So?" I said after opening it and not seeing anything unusual on the first page.

"Keep turning."

I did and couldn't believe it. There, at the end, was a scribble and comment from Bob. He'd read the book and liked it.

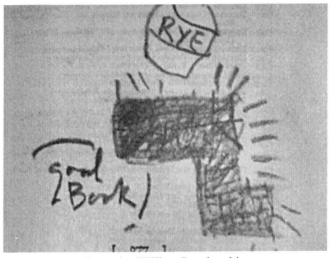

-From the William Pagel archives-

Bob explained that his participation in the making of "Pat Garrett and Billy the Kid" in Mexico in 1971 was not very satisfactory. He had young children then. His personal habits were quite different than the 60's. After shooting was done for the day he felt alone in that crowd. Everyone else was apparently living it up, getting drunk, or stoned. It sometimes continued when filming started next day.

"I was disappointed in some people," he said.

The names aren't important. He wasn't being hypocritical, or judgmental. He was making an observation it wasn't where he was at then.

He brought up his differences with Albert Grossman. He felt a sense of big betrayal and was still angry about what had transpired. It wasn't the 25% Albert got as his manager that bothered him. While higher than most manager's fees, he was well aware of Albert's skills and the fact no one could make deals like Albert.

"I never had a problem with Albert's 25% management fee," he stated.

In the beginning, for all his acumen, there were certain things Bob didn't know. Once he began performing day after day all over the country, then the world, with record sales, airplay, and other people performing his songs, publishing royalties started generating very significant income. Writing and performing took an enormous physical and emotional toll. The business end of publishing royalties was completely left to Grossman. When Bob finally had the time to look into the actual mechanics of publishing he concluded he'd been badly screwed. The creative process of songwriting was his alone. It was unconscionable, he felt, that Albert, while registering each work, had allotted himself a large part of the publishing royalties. Not only was that huge money, but a breach of trust.

"He was stealing my mind," were his exact words.

It was something for which the only remedy was a separation; a dissolution of the relationship, and not very pleasant legal proceedings. In the end, the relationship was dissolved and most financial matters settled up. Yet, though it was over and he was on a new course, it was clear by his expressions it had a left an emotional scar.

He talked about his relationship with "The Band;" how they fit into his life and his feelings about various members. He explained how things were a lot more complicated and difficult than most people realized, but due to the intensely personal content of what he told us and how it might affect other people's feelings I can't disclose what was said. It was told in confidence and there it will stay unless Bob, himself, decides otherwise.

The phone rang. My mother had to excuse herself for a little while because it was Aunt Gig on the line. That gave Bob and me some time alone. When my mother returned his most important concern was put right out on the table.

" Eve, my marriage..."

What transpired then was not meant for my ears. I went into the living room closing both sets of hallway doors between it and the kitchen behind me as the conversation began. While the specific words the two voices were exchanging were not intelligible, there was no way to shut out the enveloping atmosphere of concern and some sadness…

Then, he had to leave and go wherever he was scheduled to be.

CHAPTER **32**: HARD RAIN

While my mother was on the phone with my aunt Gig during his 1973 visit I had time to talk with Bob about two early songs he had written; how they affected me and other people that heard them.

I always loved his early 1962 song "Let Me Die In My Footsteps." I saw him do it at Gerde's. When he sang the chorus on the early verses his head was cocked with his eyes focused slightly upward. When he sang the last chorus, which changed from "Let (me) die in my footsteps" to "Then (you'll) die in your footsteps," he would lean into the microphone and focus his eyes directly at the audience like an exclamation point.

(Bob's handwritten chorus for every verse except the last one)

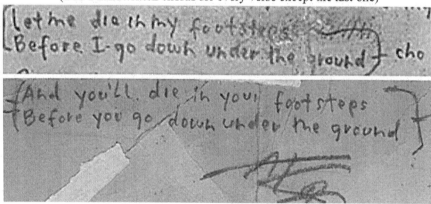

(Bob's handwritten chorus to the last verse)

His record company had never officially released it. I asked him if they ever would.

"I don't know, Pete. That's up to them. When they released 'The Freewheelin' a few first pressings had the song on it. I had written and recorded more songs by then and they immediately pulled it. It was replaced with another song."

That brought me to my other favorite song, one of the ones that was added after the switch off from that first pressing - "A Hard Rain's A-Gonna Fall." He knew how much it affected my mother by her request to hear it when he was at our apartment on April 14, 1963. He didn't know then how the song affected me. I had immediately memorized the lyrics and guitar chords.

A month after the April 14, 1963 night Bob sang it at our apartment, near the end of my senior year in high school, through a school program, I performed at a civil rights benefit concert for C.O.R.E. (Congress of Racial Equality). It was down in the East Village right near where the Fillmore East would open 5 years later. I went with Ellie, the same girl who came with me a year later to see Bob perform in Cambridge. When we got there and checked in a young comedian was halfway through his act. People were falling off their chairs laughing. When he finished the MC went to the microphone and introduced me. Ellie and I were the only white faces in the entire place. They gave me a warm round of applause as I adjusted the microphone. I looked around the whole room, nodding to all sides. I did not want to appear rude by not acknowledging everyone there.

"Thank you. It is a real privilege to be here. I am going to do a song for you."

I took a deep breath and six minutes later finished the last notes of "A Hard Rain's A-Gonna Fall." For a moment there was a silence. Then I heard the first clap and everyone was clapping. I couldn't believe it. A nervous and relieved smile broke out on my 17-year-old face.

"Thank you very much," I said, as I got off the stage.

I went back to our table and sat down. Out of nowhere the young comedian who had performed before me came over with his hand extended to shake mine.

"Man, that was something else."

What a nice compliment. I never forgot his name. Although I never met him again I became one of the millions of Richard Pryor fans. It was then I realized I hadn't mentioned it was a song written by Bob Dylan. The point is, when a young, white, 17-year-old in 1963 sings a song to an all-black audience, a song they've never heard before, gets applause and a compliment like that, that's SOME song.

I performed "Hard Rain" publicly in 1964 at the Harvard Club in New York City. It was my first paid, professional gig. It was reviewed in the March 21, 1964 issue of the "New Yorker" magazine. The other performers were Tom Glazer, The Charles River Valley Boys and Judy Collins. We each did three songs and then an encore which was the group sing-along. Unlike the C.O.R.E. audience, being the Harvard Club, that audience was white, older, more conservative, and a lot of stuff went right over their heads. What bowled me over was when I finished my third song, Bob's "Hard Rain," Judy Collins had tears in her eyes.

"Peter, never stop singing," she said.

You could have knocked me down with a feather…

I wish I could have taken her advice. I did continue to sing and play in private, but not very often in public (except in groups).

All my life I had these little tics and sometimes made involuntary noises. I didn't think much about it because I figured it was a normal part of growing up. They were mild and I thought I would grow out of it. I didn't. The tics and sounds used to come in little bunches and then disappear for a while. Stress helped trigger it, though I was able to hide, or mask it fairly well. As I finished my teens and entered my 20's, while still mild, the tics and involuntary sounds became more regular. I became more reserved in public. While it may not always have been that noticeable to others, it distressed me. I was very sensitive about it. When I went for regular doctors' visits they never commented on it. I continued mainly focusing on my art. Art is a solitary thing and all that matters is the finished image itself. It wasn't until my mid 40's that a physician in New York City commented on the tics and noises and sent me to a specialist. It turned out I had what is known as "Tourette's Syndrome." It's a neurological disorder that causes, among other things, involuntary sounds and twitching. Some people have it much worse than I do. That's for another time and a longer discussion. It can render some virtually incapable of functioning if undiagnosed, or misdiagnosed.

Fortunately, there are exercise channelings and medications that can do wonders. There are also support groups. So, if you have any of the symptoms like mine, or, as parents, see any of your children with similar symptoms, go to a doctor as soon as possible and explain the concerns. There is help out there that can change the direction of lives. If only one person is helped by reading this, or made aware this condition exists and is treatable, I will consider this book a success, whatever you might think of the rest of it.

I performed "Hard Rain" in public at the club 47 in Cambridge in the spring of 1966, my junior year in college. It was a special radio broadcast. I did it solo while two of my friends sat behind me on stage. When I finished one of them went to the piano and the other picked up a second guitar. We kicked into an up-tempo blues rock song we had put together, similar to "High Heeled Sneakers."

I was on rhythm guitar with the harmonica rig around my neck. When we got off stage this fellow came over and said:

"You play one hell of a mean harp (harmonica)."

"Thank you very much," I replied. "I was lucky. I had a great teacher."

A couple of years later I was in a record store thumbing through albums. There, on a record jacket, was a picture of the man who'd complimented me. His name was Taj Mahal.

When I finished telling Bob about the occasions I performed "Hard Rain" he looked at me and said in a quiet voice:

"I always knew you had it in you."

I was about to say something else when my mother came back in the kitchen and the moment passed.

Twenty-nine years later I was on the phone with Stephen Brown, one of the Harvard friends who had played with me that day at the Club 47. I hadn't talked to him in 20 years.

"I'm writing a book about my family's relationship with Bob Dylan," I told him.

His reply was unexpected. He told me he wrote articles three or four times a year for the "Times Literary Supplement," London. On January 7, 2011, they printed one of his pieces. It was a review of a new Dylan biography.

"I first listened to a Bob Dylan album in the bedroom of a girl from Long Island. "You've got to hear this," she said, taking me away from our older relatives, and playing music pretty much the way it was introduced to Sean Wilentz, "as if it were a piece of just-revealed scripture." I listened, and then, torn between wanting to seem cool and wanting to seem honest, plumped for honesty. "It's kind of out of tune, isn't it?" I could see all respect for me slowly drain from her eyes.

Just a few months later, in my freshman dorm room, I sat enthralled as my friend Pete McKenzie pounded out all the many verses to "A Hard Rain's A-Gonna Fall". The boots with which he stamped that time were, he said with reverence, Bob Dylan's own, left behind at the Mackenzie family apartment."

My 50th High School of Music and Art class reunion took place in NYC in June 2013. Emails to a general discussion group were exchanged between class members leading up to the event. I decided to share a story few of my classmates were aware of.

In the Fall of 1962, the beginning of high school senior year, I was elected as an officer of the student body on a campaign promise to bring folksingers to perform at the school.

"Bobby, I just got elected to the student body," I told him.

"Congratulations, Pete."

"Thing is, I promised to bring folk singers to perform for the school. Would you do it?"

"Sure. Just tell me when. If there's no scheduling conflict I'll be there."

I went to the faculty adviser for approval. I figured it was just a formality. She asked only one question.

"Does he wear a tie?"

"He normally doesn't," I answered truthfully.

"That's unfortunate. Since he doesn't wear a tie he can't perform for us," she curtly replied.

AND SO, BOB DYLAN WAS NOT ALLOWED TO PERFORM AT OUR SCHOOL.

Once I emailed that story to my reunion classmates it was all I could do to keep the computer from heartburn.

Elizabetta D.:

"Pete, noooooooooooooooooo. Give me 5 minutes with that teacher."

Rosemarie P.:

"Elizabetta, can you spare me just one of those five minutes? This is why there was the Sixties."

Ellen S.:

"Oh, Peter, now I know what might have been, I'm so disappointed. As for the small world it continues to be, a former partner of mine grew up in Hibbing, MN. Her older sister went to Hebrew school with Bobbie Zimmerman and was kicked out of the school after Bobbie told the rabbi to go "fuck himself" and she laughed. Perhaps he'd remember the anecdote. I guess he was always a rebel."

There were many more.

The last one was from Gail Gutradht.

"Your story of the aborted Dylan concert cries for a personal reply. I remember one day at school when you brought your guitar and sang for the class, "Hard Rain". It was the first Dylan song I ever heard and it floored me. I ran out and bought 'Freewheeling'. When I played it at home my brother, five years and so many generations older, whose current politics are still somewhere to the right of Attila the Hun, made cruel fun of Dylan's singing, and of me for spending money on such an obvious loser. It became almost impossible to play in the house when anyone was home, but I was off to the races. Not only did I follow Dylan for all those years, but "Hard Rain" was also my introduction to the Child Ballads as well, from which that song borrows so much inspiration. Such beautiful words and today I am a writer. Who knows where these things begin? So you see, Peter, although for want of a necktie the concert was lost, you channeled your inner Bob Dylan, and I have remembered your concert with gratitude many times over the last 50 years. How sweet to finally have an opportunity to thank you for it!"

I was at a loss for words.

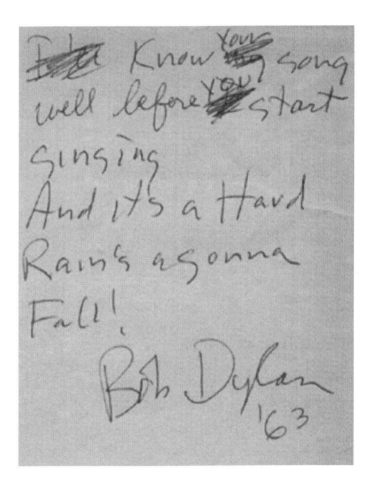

CHAPTER 33: IT'S ALL IN THE FEET

My parents' friends, Duke and Millie Livingston always had a thing about proper footwear. You could look any way you wanted, but you had to have a proper pair of shoes. In late 1962 they thought the pair of suede boots Bob always wore were starting to look worn out. One evening when Bob was visiting 28th St. Millie and Duke came over with a brand-new pair of boots; the same model as Bob's worn pair. He tried them on, and they fit perfectly. Bob is wearing those boots on the cover of the "Freewheelin' Bob Dylan," where he's walking down the street, arm in arm with Suze Rotolo. He was very appreciative of his new footgear. They went everywhere with him, on stage and off. The old pair? Bob and I were the same shoe size. They went into my closet, to be brought out again in early 1963, the final semester of my senior year.

Duke and Millie visited us again at the apartment in April 1963 before they moved permanently to San Mateo, California. On that April day Bob again was there. Everyone was in an upbeat mood, and it was one of those moments when everything — no one could describe it better than Millie herself. These are her words from the affidavit she wrote and signed in 1993.

"My husband, Duke, and I moved from NYC to San Francisco on May 1, 1963. A short time earlier, I visited the McKenzies with Duke in NYC, who were old friends. During that visit, Bob Dylan stopped by. He went into the kitchen to eat a cheese sandwich, sat down at the kitchen table and started to write. I looked in on him a few minutes later and he was still working away. He hadn't come in the apartment with a guitar, but I saw a black guitar case laying against the kitchen table. He came into the living room shortly thereafter, guitar in hand, and asked us to listen to what he had just composed. I still remember the sound of those steel strings as he sang some verses and the chorus of a song later to be known as "It Ain't Me, Babe." He was having fun, shaking his hips a little, so I stood behind him and shook my hips, too, and we sang the chorus together. He was still wearing the boots my husband, Duke, had given him the year before, the same ones he is wearing on the cover of the album, The Freewheeling Bob Dylan."

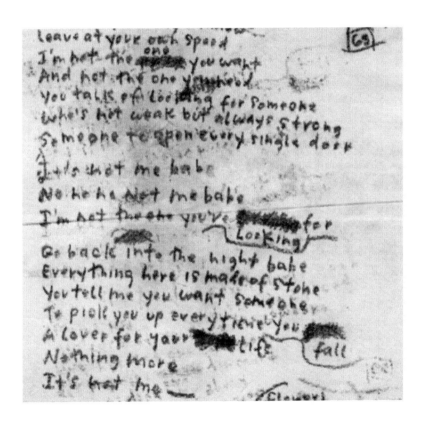

(Millie's affidavit)

My husband, Duke, and I, moved from N.Y.C. to San Francisco on May 1, 1963. A short time earlier in 1963, I visited the McKenzies with Duke in N.Y.C., who were old friends. During that visit Bob Dylan stopped by. He went into the kitchen to eat a cheese sandwich, sat down at the kitchen table and started to write. I looked in on him a few minutes later and he was still working away. He didn't come in the apartment with a guitar, but I saw a black guitar case laying on the kitchen table. He came into the living room shortly thereafter, guitar in hand, and asked me to listen to what he had just composed. I still remember the sound of those steel strings as he sang some verses and the chorus of a song later to be known as "It ain't Me Babe." He was having fun, shaking his hips a little, so I stood beside him & shook my hips too and we sang the chorus together. He was still wearing the boots that my husband, Duke, had given him the year before, the same ones he is wearing on the cover of the album, <u>The Freewheelin' Bob Dylan</u>.

Sworn before me on 6/11/93

Mildred Livingston

June 11, 1993

FRANCIS McMANUS
Notary Public, State of New York
No. ...

It turns out those original boots Bob gave me after Duke and Millie had given him a new pair held more karma than I realized.

As I got involved in writing this book I remembered the name, Ann Lauterbach. She had been mentioned somewhere in connection with a trip Bob made to Madison, Wisconsin, in late

1960. There was an Ann Lauterbach who had become an internationally recognized poet, as well as a professor at Bard College in New York. Leon Botstein, the long-serving president of Bard, had been one of my good friends in high school. There also had been a classmate of mine in elementary school named David Lauterbach. We would constantly be going to each other's apartments when we were kids. David had an older sister named Ann who had gone to our elementary school, and then to the same high school as me. I hadn't spoken with David since 1959. This was a great excuse to reconnect, and maybe get some questions answered. After searching I located his number and called him. We had a wonderful conversation. It was as if we had last seen each other the day before. I told him I was writing a book without mentioning the name of the artist who was my subject. I teasingly said:

"Here's a hint. Ann Lauterbach and a famous musician in the 60's."

"Oh, your book is about Bob Dylan," he exclaimed.

It was the same Ann, David's older sister. She was also that poet. David told me the story...

"When my sister was a freshman at the University of Wisconsin, Madison in 1960 she was befriended by a nineteen-year-old from Minnesota named Bob Dylan. He wound up staying with her and her boyfriend at their apartment off campus. She liked him; he would sit on top of the upright piano playing harmonica. Ann noticed that his footwear wasn't in the best condition for the Wisconsin cold. She had some spare money and bought him a pair of suede boots.

After a moment of silence, I said to David:

"Can you ask Ann how much I owe her for the boots?"

"What do you mean?"

"Well, it's the least I can do since I wore them all through my freshman year in college."

I told him the whole story and when we hung up I started to think about the concept of fate. We didn't know the name Bob Dylan in 1960, and yet his first pair of boots were given to him by a friend of the McKenzies. Then he got his second pair of boots, which he wore up through part of 1964, also from a family friend of the McKenzies. The odds that the first two pairs of boots Bob wore walking to fame would come from friends of the McKenzies were astronomical.

(Bob's first pair of boots)

(Bob's second pair of boots)

CHAPTER 34:
FIVE DAYS IN '62 AND ONE IN '63

The first few months of 1962 were important to Bob. Five days, in particular, stood out for me...

January 27, 1962 was a celebratory day. It was only one year earlier Bob first set foot on the pavement in New York City, completely unknown, with only the clothes on his back. Now, here he was with a signed recording deal on a major label and a record album soon to be released. He'd had several important performing engagements, glowing written reviews, more songs in his arsenal from writing nonstop; and he had signed a lease to move into his own apartment on Bleecker St.

He was sitting on our couch in the early evening looking forward to that official release and anxious to share some of his new material. Bob looked over at my father:

"Which one should I do?" he asked.

Before anyone could answer, he said:

"I'll just do a couple, OK?"

"Sure," Dad replied.

Bob looked at me as I got up to get him my guitar.

"I promise I'll come over sometime during the week because I'll be in town," he said.

I showed him the flat picks in my hand so he could use one to strum the guitar strings.

"You want to use this one?" I asked.

He looked at my outstretched palm.

"That's cool," he said.

"No, this one," I replied.

"Which one?" he asked.

"They're your picks. This is your pick," I said pointing at one.
"Is this the one I gave you?"
"No," I answered.
"Oh, this is the one. Oh, geez, from before?"
"Yeah, that's yours," I nodded
"Is this one yours?" he asked pointing to another one.
"Yeah yeah, that's the one," I replied.
"Yeah, this is a good one. This is the kind I usually use."
"This is a horrible one. I hate this one," I parried, pointing at the offender.
"It is?" he exclaimed.

It was starting to sound like an Abbott and Costello sketch. I put them all in his hand so he could decide which one was best. He started pressing each pick against his leg to determine their stiffness.

"This one's too soft."
"Too soft?" I said.
"Yeah. Steel strings. It's great for this one, though."

My guitar had nylon strings and Bob had now made his choice which pick would be most appropriate. He handed me back the rest. By the look on my face he could see I was expecting him to start right off now that he had the pick.

"Wait, wait. Let me tune it first."

He decided to do two songs. The first one was called "Hard Times From The Country Living Down In New York Town." Bob was looking up from time to time enjoying the fact we were enjoying it. It was a lighthearted ode to NYC. Then, before he started the next song, his whole body shifted. When he began to sing it was clear why…

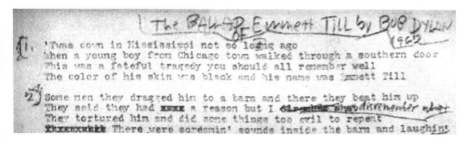

It was one he had just written, and we were the first to hear it. Though I've heard him sing it many times since, no performance had the raw power of that first time. He called it "The Ballad of Emmett Till."

On February 23, 1962, there was a group concert at City College. Bob did a set. Jack Elliott did a set. A fellow I was not yet familiar with, Len Chandler, did a set. Len was very involved in the civil rights scene at the time and continues to be politically active to this day.

The concert was a raucous affair in a gymnasium auditorium. No stage, just a flat floor, completely full of City College students and others. It was a couple blocks north of our high school. I was sitting about 30 feet from the mike, on the side, against the wall, on a long wooden bench, everyone crammed together. My friends and I were making as much noise clapping and cheering in between songs as we could. The best part was afterward because no one had made plans what to do. Bob looked at Jack. Jack looked at Len. Len at Bob. Then Jack and Bob both looked at me.

"28th St. Let's go see Eve and Mac. Len, you've gotta meet them," they said at the same time.

I called my parents from a pay phone to make sure it was okay.

"Of course," they both said. "Bring the boys on down."

Down we went. Jack was a little tired, so he was initially quiet, sitting in one of the living room chairs. I think he fell asleep a couple of times with his cowboy hat over his eyes. Len was sitting on the other living room wicker chair opposite the couch. Bob and I were sitting on the couch next to each other and we started playing a duet. The tape recorder was on. I was playing rhythm guitar and singing lead with Bob doing the harmony and playing lead guitar on an old Carter family song called "Bury Me Beneath The Willow." He was getting a hoot out of it. You can imagine how I was feeling as he kept on encouraging me. Bob was so good at harmonizing and coming up with lead guitar riffs on the instrumental parts. I only knew one verse, so I said:

"Bobby, you want me to keep going?"

"Do you know any more verses?"

"No," I replied.

"Well, I don't know any more verses. You sing the verses."

"But I only know one," I answered.

"Oh... sing it again."

So, I did. We kept going and really stretched it out.

I put down my guitar after that one song. I just wanted to watch Bob play. He started doing an Elvis Presley tune called "That's All Right, Mama." I really liked it, but Bob misunderstood my look and stopped.

"You don't like that one?"

Before I could answer he started another song, "Wayfaring Stranger," an old traditional ballad, but with a bluesy twist. I'd never heard it done like that. It sure wasn't traditional. It sounded like a different song.

Len and Bob started talking, fiddling with their guitars. Their conversation overlapped.

Bob - "That ain't it... I..."

Len - "That's it..."

Bob - "I didn't do that, man... I don't remember that..."

Len - "That was at the end of the phrase..."

Their interchange was getting a little confusing, but Bob put an end to it by breaking into a song about a train.

When he was done, he leaned back:

"I'm tired, man. I'm too tired," putting the guitar aside.

He had something to drink and talked a bit with Len. The play pause gave him a second wind. He picked the guitar back up and started strumming. It sounded like a song I thought I had heard before.

"This 'New York Town'?" I asked.

"Nah," he said.

He began something called "It Makes A Long Time Man Feel Bad." Len joined in on the harmony and it sounded great.

Jack began to stir. I could see his eyes emerging from under his hat. If you listen to the opening of "Bob Dylan's 115th Dream" on his 1965 album, "Bringing It All Back Home," there is a false start, laughter from someone in the control room, then a restart. I was watching Bob, so I wasn't sure if it was Jack who was the instigator. But, either Jack, Len, or both, started to tease him in the middle of his rendition by making funny faces and hand gestures. Whatever they did they had his number because he started laughing through the last words of one line before starting the next one. Their antics got to him. He tried his best to finish the song... he didn't succeed. He was laughing so much through each word of the next line he couldn't coordinate the chords. The guitar playing stopped. He cracked up uncontrollably, but deeper and longer than the laugh of the person in that control room. Len and Jack both appeared self-satisfied as Bob couldn't stop laughing. My parents were standing behind Jack and Len. My mother looked at my father, then looked at Bob, shaking her head.

"Look at those three. They're like children."

I was disappointed because Bob never got to finish the song.

"You like that?" Bob said after he managed to stop laughing.

Len spoke up:

"Hey, Dylan... I want to sing. I want to sing... my words to '500 miles.' Play that 'cause... that was fun to do."

Bob had something else in mind, though.

"Wait. Wait. Here's another one. It's called 'I Was Riding Number Nine'... This grows."

It sure did.

He started out quietly on the first verse. As he began the second Len asked:

"Did you write that?"

Bob didn't answer. He kept on going. Then the song started to build in tension. By the time he got to the climax of the last chorus he was wailing. When he hit the last chord, he let out an Elvis like, "Yeaaaah..."

Everyone laughed at the growl.

"You like that?" he asked with a broadening smile.

Now there are a few things about that song you should know. I found out later it was written by Hank Williams. The real title is "Lonesome Whistle Blues." Though the words were the same, because of the way Bob arranged it you wouldn't immediately recognize that. The best way to describe his performance; it's the only other song I've heard him do that builds like "House Of The Rising Sun," from his first album.

Hopefully, sometime, all the 28th St. recordings will become available, publicly, made from the ORIGINAL master tapes. When he was there with us at home, feeling comfortable and uninhibited, spontaneously performing, his voice had a depth and quality not heard before, or since.

On March 19, 1962, Bob's first record on Columbia titled "Bob Dylan" was officially released to the public. The real commotion for us happened a little earlier. We didn't know the exact release date, or which specific songs would be on it. A few days before it's official debut Bob called up.

"Can I come over?"

Half an hour later he arrived with Suze, bursting with overflowing energy, enthusiasm and pride.

"We did it," he said. "Here it is," as he pulled out a couple of record albums from under his arm.

"Here it is. My first record."

"Congratulations. We're so proud of you. You deserve it," my parents exclaimed.

"Where's the record player?" Bob asked.

We had this little portable record player. It was the kind you carry around with the handle. When you want to play something, you open it up, put it on the table, plug it in and the sound comes out through little built-in speakers on each side. It sounded pretty good. There was only one small hitch. A couple of weeks earlier something in it broke and we hadn't had a chance to fix it. Of all the rotten luck. Here was the big moment. THE BIG MOMENT.

Frantically thinking I said, "I have an idea. "I'll go downstairs and get Howard. He has a professional stereo system, and we can all listen to it there. It'll be great."

I rushed out of the apartment, ran downstairs and knocked on Howard's door. No answer. I knocked again.

"Howard," I yelled.

Still no answer.

I walked back upstairs.

"He's not home."

Everyone was sitting down. Bob looked up. He could feel my agitation. He'd come rushing over to share his accomplishment. He sensed I felt I let him down. Why was the record player still broken? Why hadn't I taken it to be fixed? If only I hadn't used it so much it would be working now...

"Don't worry, Pete. I'll leave the records here. As soon as you can get to a record player let me know what you think."

After they left I felt pretty low. I looked at the front cover, then the back cover, then the front cover again, then the back cover. I messed around with the little record player to see if there was anything I could figure out that would fix it, even if only for a few minutes, so we could hear something. Anything! It was fruitless. We would have to wait. Howard HAD to get home sometime. Each time I thought I heard a noise on the staircase my ears pricked up, only to be let down. Finally, there was a heavier sound on the lower stairs. I bolted out of the apartment, record it hand, and looked over the railing. It was Howard unlocking his front door.

"Howard," I shouted, waiving the album.

He was startled for a second.

"Whoa, Pete, what's going on?"

"Bobby and Suze came over today with Bobby's album. Our record player is broken. Can we come down?"

"Hold on a minute, Pete. I can see you're excited. Let me get myself situated first. Give me 15 minutes to unpack my gear."

I knew he wanted to hear it as well. Bob had certainly spent enough time in his apartment with Anne-Marie and him.

15 minutes. I kept looking at the mantle clock. As soon as the second hand went around the 15th time I was out the door, with my folks walking slowly behind. Howard's door was open, so I went in and headed straight for the stereo system. He heard me and stuck his head out of the kitchen. His apartment had a different layout than ours. He had done a lot of renovation and opened up

the whole place. It was now like a big loft with the kitchen and bedroom off to the side.

"Hold up there, Pete. I'll do it. It's a very sensitive system."

I saw his point. In my haste I might have accidentally mauled everything. I stopped and waited until he came out of the kitchen. When he did I handed him the album. He looked at the front and back cover, then carefully took out the record. He got a cloth to wipe the disc off making sure there was no dust on it. He wiped off the turntable and gently placed the side labeled "A" face up. He turned on the preamp, then the amp, set the equalizer and volume, and slightly adjusted the wall mounted speakers. As he finished my parents arrived downstairs. Howard had set up two chairs for them right in the middle of the room. They sat down.

"Everyone all set?" asked Howard.

He clicked the turntable on, waited a couple of seconds to make sure it was up to proper speed. He positioned the turntable arm over the grooves of the first track and placed the needle gently on it. The record revolved around a couple of times with the usual static crackle…

The first guitar chords started roaring through the speakers. Hardly a word was spoken for the first 20 minutes. Howard turned the record over and side "B" played for another 20 minutes. As soon as the last note was heard the record player automatically clicked off.

"Well, I'm glad to see he took some of my advice," Howard wryly remarked.

He liked Bob and they enjoyed talking with each other. He had taken great early photos of Bob and Bob had gone through his entire record collection, which was extensive. One day Bob came into his apartment and played a song he'd written wanting his feedback.

"The song is really good, but stop singing like Woody Guthrie and let your own voice come through," Howard told him.

Bob immediately barked back:

"What do you know about music."

If you knew Howard, his comment about the record made sense.

You didn't ask him for feedback if you only wanted praise. He spoke his mind. It did appear, though, Bob had somewhat listened.

As for not knowing about music, in mid-1970 I dropped by Howard's, and he played me a record of a new artist he said was going to be huge. It didn't particularly grab me at the time, but he was entitled to his opinion. The artist?... Elton John.

Bob's album was a surprise. It sounded very different than I thought it would. I was familiar with all the songs and how they sounded before. This was the first time I'd heard his voice for that long on a professional recording using state of the art tape machines, special microphones, reverb and no background noise. I was used to hearing him live, or on home recordings.

We called Bob and Suze the next day. He was amused when I had to be pried away from the phone while using every adolescent word of praise and accolade I could think of.

(Bob and Suze's phone number in Mom's brass desk pad)
-From the William Pagel archives-

(Bob's first album inscribed)

As enthusiastic as I was talking to Bob about his first album it was equaled to what occurred a month later.

The date was April 24, 1962. Bob was no longer the undercard at Gerde's. He was the headliner and we had complimentary house tickets. Since I was accompanied by my folks there was no problem with my age. I told as many of my high school friends as I could and some managed to get in. The place was full up. The stage light came on and Bob started to play a set that lasted about 40 minutes. He told funny stories in between numbers, had everyone laughing, clapping, yelling, whistling. In between one of the songs my mother who was standing back near the bar was talking to John Lee Hooker. As I eavesdropped, I heard John Lee say:

"That's our boy up there."

It was only a year ago Bob had rushed through our apartment door before his first paying Gerde's engagement saying:

"I'm on the same bill with John Lee Hooker. He's the man."

Now here was the man himself saying, "That's our boy up there."

Bob was playing some songs I had never heard before. When he came off stage he walked to the back of the bar, near the kitchen, where I had stationed myself and stood next to me.

"Hey, Pete, glad to see you," he said as the bartender slid him a shot of scotch. I see your mom is talking to John Lee."

"Yeah," I replied, then told him what I heard John Lee tell her.

"Really?" he said.

"Yeah," I answered. "You did some new stuff. That 'Blowing in the Wind' number, when did you write that?"

"Oh, a little while ago. I did it here last week to see how it would go over. The audience liked it. I'm thinking of putting it on my next album."

"Your next album? You're already doing another one? The first one just came out."

"I know," Bob said. "I've been writing a lot of new things and I want to get them down. In fact, it's been a long day. I had my first session at Columbia this afternoon and I've got another scheduled for tomorrow. But, keep it to yourself."

"What did you record?" I asked.

"I did a couple of different takes of 'Emmett Till'."

"That's the one you did at the apartment a couple of months ago."

"Oh, yeah," he replied. "I had just written it and I wanted your folks to hear it."

"It really impressed them," I said.

Bob paused for a second then motioned to the bartender.

As he downed his second shot of scotch he told him, "Give my friend a soda."

"Thanks, Bobby."

"No problem, Pete. Listen, the next set is going to begin soon. Let me say 'hi' to your mom and dad before it starts."

"OK. See you later."

As he left I saw my high school friend, Peggy Goodwin. She was a senior and going out with a college freshman, so she had no trouble getting in. She was an early Bob fan, and it wasn't just because his first album included the song "Pretty Peggy-O." I started to make my way over to her as random chatter filled the air. Simultaneously, I had my eye out trying to locate Suze.

(Gerde's schedule sign in log book, April 1962 - From the William Pagel archives)

On a Sunday, at the beginning of June, my father and I were walking around Washington Square Park. Coming towards us, arm in arm, were Bob and Suze. She was beaming as usual, and Bob looked quite the dude. He was wearing a brand-new vest. Very sharp. We hadn't seen them in a month. To me that seemed like a year. I hugged them both. Dad and Bob shook hands and Suze gave Dad a big kiss on the cheek.

"How's the young Harvard man?" were the first words out of Bob's mouth.

"I haven't sent out the application, yet."

"Aww, just details," he replied.

"You know," I told him, "I'm going to work for my cousin, Larry, at his design firm next summer."

Larry was more like an uncle than cousin.

"Ahh, the young architect," he mused.

"By the way, how is Leslie?" he asked.

Leslie was the one who'd given me my first guitar, and was Larry's wife.

"She's fine. She always asks about you and how you're doing."

Both she and Larry had been over to our apartment when Bob was there, and she and Bob got along like a house on fire. I think he had a crush on her though he would never admit it.

"Suze and I are going to walk around the fountain," he announced.

"We'll go with you," I said.

All four of us started walking. It was a nice, wind free day. There were small clusters of people gathered around various groups. We noticed a crowd larger than the rest.

"Let's take a look over there," says Bob.

We get there and no wonder the crowd is larger. Right in the center under a cowboy hat is Jack Elliott.

"Hey Jack," Bob shouts.

He starts making his way through the crowd. I wasn't far behind. My father and Suze were content to stand on the outside. It didn't seem there was much jostling. A few people recognize Bob and step aside. He gets to the opening in the middle.

"Hey, Bob, you got any harps with you?" Jack asks.

Bob rummages around in the pockets of his vest.

Out come a couple of harmonicas.

"What keys are they in?"

"Don't know. Let me see."

Bob checks them.

"Ok," says Jack, sliding his capo up a couple of frets. "Let's do

'Mule Skinner Blues'."

You could hear Jack's guitar and voice, along with Bob's harmonica and chiming in on vocal harmonies. When the next song started Suze and Dad were no longer on the outside of the crowd. They'd become surrounded by people as the crowd continued to grow. You could hear the whispers:

"That's Bob Dylan and Jack Elliott," or "Jack Elliott and Bob Dylan."

The name order didn't matter to me. I had the best spot on the planet. Had my dad and I come down the following Sunday instead, we would not have seen a sharply dressed harmonica player walking arm in arm with his paramour. A week later Suze was hundreds of miles away, on an ocean liner, bound for Italy.

In February 1963 I was with my friend, Marilyn, down in the village on Bleecker Street. I was wearing the boots Bob had given me when Duke and Millie had given him a new pair. As we turned a corner we almost collided with a couple walking as fast as possible down the street as the snow on the ground would allow. They were bundled up. It was a cold morning.

"Hi, Bobby," I said.

"Oh, hi Pete."

Suze was with him.

"What brings you down here?" he asked. "Who is your friend?"

I introduced everyone.

"We're just walking around. Nothing special," I told him. "How about the two of you?"

"We're going back to our apartment to straighten it up. There's a photographer coming over this afternoon to do some promo shots of Bobby for Columbia. His new album is going to be out soon, and they want some photos," Suze said.

"His new album?" I exclaimed, with the same surprise I had the previous April.

"Yes. I've been doing a lot of writing and recording of only my own songs. They're different than the ones before. You're going to really like them. So will your folks," Bob replied.

"Will it include "Let Me Die In My Footsteps?" I asked.

"Not sure. There's a lot of new material."

I noticed his boots. I shifted my weight so my left leg was forward.

"Look," I said, "we have matching boots."

"You're right," he said with a laugh. "They look good on you. But, now we have to get moving. Say hi to your folks and tell them I'll stop by soon. Nice meeting you, Marilyn," he added as the two of them turned to get back to their house tidying.

Bob's "Freewheelin" album came out two months later with a photo of Bob and Suze arm and arm on the cover. There was snow on the ground. Suze was wearing the same clothes in the photo from that morning. It turned out it was that afternoon on Jones Street the photo for the cover was taken. Bob, though, was not wearing the same outfit from the morning. He had changed into a light weight, almost summer jacket, and it was the dead of winter. He was still wearing those boots.

"Weren't you freezing?" I later asked him after the album was released..

"I'm used to the cold, Pete, and besides, it's show business."

Then he winked.

CHAPTER 35:
NOVEMBER 23, 1961 - ANYTHING BUT A TURKEY

Rumors over the years have it that Bob felt a degree of disappointment regarding his performance on his first publicly released album. He felt he could have done better. Everything was too rushed, too mechanical. If only he could have a do-over...

Fortunately, it is something he no longer needs to be concerned about. He never had to. The redo has been around all this time. All that remains is go back to November 23, 1961, to a familial setting in a 4th floor walkup apartment.

When people talk about family and friends getting together to celebrate just being alive, Thanksgiving, 1961 is as good as it gets. And it's all captured on audiotape; audio so clear you feel as though you are physically there - as a participant.

The day started off normally like any other day. Anne-Marie came up from downstairs in the morning to talk with my mother about what needed to be prepared. Soon after Anne-Marie went back downstairs my father and I helped arrange the furniture so people could move around more easily, and have a place to sit. I helped get the plates, forks, knives and glasses ready. It was pretty much a BYOB affair, so only a couple of bottles of the hard stuff were on hand. My aunt, Gig, arrived a little after noon. While my mother was cooking Gig looked over the apartment.

"You've done a nice job, Peter, but some of the chairs should be moved here and the shelves need more dusting. I'm going into the kitchen to help your mother."

As 1 pm turned to 2 pm, then 3 pm, I was getting a little antsy. I had an idea who was going to come, but didn't know when, for how long, or who they would bring. When I heard some noises in the hallway I looked out the front door. There were people going upstairs to the Neals and Pearsons. I followed them to wish Hank and his wife, as well as Mommy Dorcas and her daughters, little Dorcas and Sharon, a wonderful holiday. They were cooking as well. I went back downstairs and got my first overall impression how everything would appear when a guest entered. It looked neat, clean, everything in place. What really struck me right then was the work my parents had put into the apartment over the years. They had exposed the red brick wall on one side of the living room. My father crafted the folding doors for their bedroom entrance. There were the doors they had put for the hallway entrance which separated the living room from the kitchen. They had converted the small back room from a kitchen into my bedroom and the dining room into a dining room/kitchen. They had painstakingly pared down two of the kitchen walls to expose the brick underneath. My father specially constructed sliding doors for the back bedroom. The non-working fireplace was now a spice and glass storage area. There was the beautiful chest my aunt had custom designed for my parent's bedroom. Bob commented on that chest many times.

"It's fabulous," he said.

There were three homemade rugs made by my mother. The dumbwaiter had been removed in the kitchen and filled with beams laying down a floor. Dad, with Hank's help from upstairs, did it. It added extra space and it's where they put the new refrigerator Kevin got us for next to nothing from his father's construction business. There was the dark brown, 4-foot diameter heavy oak table where Bob had written many of his early songs. My folks had gotten it from the two dancers who moved out from the apartment downstairs years before. There were the homemade stools my father had made to sit on around the kitchen table. I looked at the kitchen rocking chair my grandfather had given as a gift to my parents right after I was born. Avril's drawings were framed on the living room wall, as well as some of my own paintings. The couch against the living room wall next to the door entrance Bob had slept on the entire summer was freshly vacuumed. The wonderful, long coffee table in front of the couch had been polished. I could go on, but that was enough to see my parents in a different, even more impressive light. They had taken an ordinary walk-up apartment in what was an outwardly nondescript looking building and turned it into an intimate palace. It was what no one would expect entering a building like that. It had the sense of elegance money can't buy.

I closed the front door and decided to sit in a chair in the living room for a few minutes while my mother, father and aunt were in the kitchen finishing up some last touches. There is a knock on the front door, and it opens. The first person arrives. Bob looks chipper and is by himself.

"Hey, everybody, Bobby's here."

"Hi, Pete," he says, as I jump out of the chair to give him a handshake.

Out from the kitchen come Mom, Gig and Dad.

"Sit down. Want something to drink?" says my father.

"Sure."

I couldn't believe my luck. I was going to get him all alone before everyone else started showing up.

"Where's Suze?" my mother asks.

"She'll be here later. She had some last-minute things to do."

"That's good," Mom says. "It's always nice to have her here. Oh, and Anne-Marie is downstairs doing some cooking and will be up shortly."

Dad brings out some hors d'oeuvres and something for him to drink, putting it on the coffee table. Bob is now sitting on the couch.

"Everything okay getting your new place?" my father asks.

"Yeah. Bleecker Street, it looks good."

Before Dad can say another word, I interrupt:

"Bobby, I've got something really cool to show you. Since you were here last time Mom went out and got this great tape recorder. It's a Telefunken with two microphones. I can record my guitar and listen back."

"So that's what that thing on the table is," he replies.

"Yeah. Wanna to see how it works?"

"Sure."

I take the cover off the top and bring the two microphones out from underneath the coffee table.

"It's stereo. And the quality is really good."

"Looks interesting," he says, surveying it.

"Yeah. Mom got it a short time ago."

"You already told me."

I had a one-track mind. I was dying to try it out with him. My guitar was in the corner and there was another Kevin had dropped off the day before.

"So it produces a good sound?" Bob asks.

"Yeah, it's a very good sound. It feels like you're actually there."

I put on a 5" reel of tape and the microphones on their little stands on either side of the machine.

"If you put the microphones apart it really gives a nice stereo effect. If you put one of the mikes on a couple of books, the guitar is level with one mike and the other mike is face level and you get great sound separation."

"Really?" he says, acting as if he's hearing something he doesn't already know.

"Here, I'll show you," as I turn it on, press record and the tape starts going. I speak into the microphone:

"Testing one, two, three."

I pick up my guitar and play a few chords and sing a verse of a song. I didn't complete the song; I was so anxious to show him how good the sound was. I stopped the recording, rewound the tape and played it back. It's always difficult to determine how accurate the sound is when you're the one on tape because you don't have a real idea what you sound like to others.

"You know, you're right. For a home machine the sound is very good. It sounds exactly like you," he says.

"Really?"

"Yeah. I've heard a lot of home tape recorders, and this is about the best one I've heard," he assures me.

"Want to do something together?"

"Sure," he says

"How about San Francisco Bay Blues?"

"Okay. You sing and play it," he answers. "I'll do the harmony."

I make sure not to sit too close to the microphones because I didn't want the sound to be distorted. I press the 'record' button and sing "San Francisco Bay Blues" all the way through with Bob coming in on vocals at the appropriate times.

"Let's listen back," I exclaim.

We listen... His interest is piqued.

"Pete, could you bring me that other guitar over there and I'll do something, and we'll see what it sounds like."

He takes a sip of his drink and a bite of the hors d'oeuvres.

As he tunes the guitar and is about to play I remember he has already signed with Columbia. I didn't want to get him in trouble.

"I'll erase the tape when you're through. I'll play it back and then I'll erase it so they can't say that I'm recording, you know, at Columbia, or anything."

"You can," says Bob.

"I can?"

"Yeah, you can have it."

He starts to play a song called "In My Time of Dying."

"You like that?" he says when he finishes.

I'd been watching how his fingers plucked the strings. No one else did it like that. I had to ask:

"Do you have... do you, do by any chance, have double jointed fingers? Because I notice when you play, whenever I play, you know, I always go like this."

I make a gesture showing him.

"When you play, you always go like this."

I try to imitate his finger movement as best I can.

"Do you notice that? Look at your fingers when you play."

He plays a couple of strings looking at his fingers.

"See what I mean?" I say. "I guess you're just naturally talented."

Bob laughs, and for some reason I think about his Carnegie Chapter Hall concert three weeks earlier.

"The day of the concert you said, remember you said on stage, 'I'll play that song at the house'?"

"What's that?" he asks.

"'Hard Travelin'."

It was one of my favorite songs at the time, written by Woody Guthrie. I had heard both Cisco Houston and Jack Elliott do it.

Bob laughs again.

"I'm holding you to it," I insist.

He did promise.

He starts doing another little intricate fingerpicking with those unique finger movements.

"Holy mackerel," my eyes opening wide.

"You like that?"

He was really grinning even more broadly. I was about to reply when there is a knock on the front door and two other people enter. That was the end of Bob all to myself. Dad does the introductions all around and brings them their hors d'oeuvres. Anne-Marie comes back upstairs with some stuffing. She flashes her big eyes at Bob as she goes into the kitchen. He loved that. The place begins to fill up.

"I'm going to bring up the turkey in a little while," Ann-Marie announces as she crosses the living room exiting the front door.

Bob and I are still sitting next to each other on the couch as more people come in. Now it is starting to look like a party, especially when the next person shows up. My mother had just come into the living room. She tells Bob, who is talking to me:

"Look who just arrived."

He turns his head as Mom greets Suze and he is off the couch in a flash. He bee lines right for her. My father goes back into the kitchen as my mother introduces Suze to everyone.

"This is Suze. She's with Bobby."

Suze and Bob are now talking. Suze looks over at me on the couch and gives a wave.

More people start to come in; Mark Eastman, who rode to New York City with Bob when he first arrived in January. He brought his guitar with him. Robbie Workoff is with his parents and his sister, Sue. Sue Workoff was Kevin's girlfriend. Now we had two Susans in the house – Bob's and Kevin's. Mark Dorenson, who later became the road manager for the Paul Butterfield blues band, has his mandolin. People start moving around as more arrive. They can't all fit in the same room. Anne-Marie finally comes back up with the turkey in hand. The living room parts so she can bring it into the kitchen for Dad to carve. I look around and it's as if half the University of Chicago is here. Bob sits back down next to me with Suze on his right, ready to have more bites of food. Everyone appears to be having a good time. Sometimes it's hard to hear what is being said. You know how it is with the sound of the buzz in a room while everyone's talking, eating, drinking. Though the atmosphere is all conversation, sooner or later someone is going to comment about all the guitars being here. Someone does and it falls to Bob to start things off. A guitar makes its way into his hands. He turns to look at me. I am sitting to his left. I immediately get up, adjust the microphones and press the record button. Suze moves over a little on the couch and I sit back down, this time between them.

"Oh, here's one. Here's a good one for you, Peter. This is a really good one. A good song, anyway."

He starts to do a number called "Baby Let Me Follow You Down" and the whole room begins to get quiet. Being 15, I really didn't know what this song was about. I do now. Later I learned he had recorded it on his first album. This is a different interpretation. He's halfway through the song, all eyes focused on him, his foot stomping, when the front door opens, and he suddenly stops playing.

"Hey, Kevin, how're you doing?" he exclaims.

There he stands, the "Grand Master" himself. He has made his entrance; Kevin's gaze goes straight to Bob.

"Hey there, baby," he says.

There's the instantaneous spark and bang between them. It is

Kevin's turn to take center stage for the ritual tug of war for the spotlight. Kevin, his Frank Sinatra persona in place, Bob quiet, letting his music do the talking. After the obligatory intros Kevin, feeling in his element, orders Bob to immediately sing his two favorite songs.

I'll play you another song," Bob answers.

"Oh no, you promised to play that one."

Kevin is emphatic.

"Here's one that's better," says Bob.

"I heard you play it at the concert, Bob," says Kevin, referring to Carnegie Chapter Hall on November 4th.

Bob starts another song.

"Fixin' To Die," he announces. "Ever hear 'Fixin' To Die'?"

Bob knows doing something else will get Kevin's goat and is pleased with himself. He's decided to make Kevin work for it. That immediately registers with Kevin. The more Bob decides to make him work for it, the more Kevin is determined to get his way.

"Play 'San Francisco Bay'," he says with a hand gesture. "Here we go. Go!"

He is insistent.

Bob starts playing the chords to the song in a very deliberate, slow, lackadaisical manner mumbling, "Well I'm walkin'…"

"C'mon," barks Kevin. "Just play 'House Of The Rising Sun' and 'Walking My Baby Down San Francisco Bay' and anything in Chicago is yours."

Bob senses frustration building up in Kevin and decides to turn it up a notch. He half-heartedly starts singing:

"Well, I'm walkin'..."

Then he abruptly stops.

"I'll do some Johnny Herald…," quickly running off a couple of bluegrass guitar licks.

Kevin does his best to ignore the challenge.

"Ready," he commands, determined not to let Bob get the better of him.

"What do you want to hear?" Bob asks, pretending to have already forgotten.

Kevin's voice becomes flat with no wiggles:

"'Walking My Baby Down San Francisco Bay' and 'House Of The Rising Sun'."

Bob knows THAT tone and knows he's drawn it out long enough. He gives me a quick look to bring me in on the act. The rhythm on the guitar starts...

Letting loose on that song would be an understatement. It was like a bunch of dinosaurs crashing the place. The sudden power... It was felt by everyone in the room. Even Suze was surprised at the intensity and force. It sounded like a whole band. Full throttle vocals, the Wham Bam driving guitar. Forget folk music. This was even beyond rock 'n roll. No one delivered the song like that before or since. Not even Bob. Then, the song is done, the momentary silence broken only by Kevin's voice:

"Now 'House Of The Rising Sun.' Now sing it with feeling. It's such a great number."

But, Bob had just tapped into some other kind of vein and wasn't about to change course. "San Francisco Bay" was only the warmup. Without a word he goes right into "You're No Good," another song on his first album. When you hear what he does on the song, on this night, you might want to call his record company and demand they replace that track with this rendition on any reissue. To my knowledge, no one outside of those fortunate enough to be there on that night, has ever heard Bob in person like this. Who knows where it came from? I don't know if he even knows. It's one of those once-in-a-lifetime things captured and preserved exactly as it happened over a half century ago.

"Hooray," claps Mom.

"Can I have any more vermouth? You got any more vermouth?" Bob asks.

"Yeah, but play 'House Of The Rising Sun', will ya," says Kevin.

"Want to hear that?" goes Bob.

This time he is no longer playing the game. He is in a different place. He notices Suze isn't on the couch.

"Where's Suze?" he says.

Kevin has just seen her get up to go to the bathroom.

"Suze, this is for you," he shouts, his voice reverberating down the hallway past the bathroom door into the kitchen.

Bob begins to play...

There is no way to verbally describe his rendition of "Rising Sun." It kept building, building, foot pounding, inside out growling. We're talking ripping out all emotional arteries in the heart. Raw, core exposed, last moment on earth kind of cry. Those six minutes in time... when you looked into his eyes - that is when he opened them - he wasn't just singing a song. He'd literally become the character in the narrative. I wish there were words in the dictionary to describe something like that. It did happen, though, and it was Bob who did it. It's hard to know if everyone, at the time, knew what they had witnessed. It was, after all, a party type atmosphere, not a spotlight on the stage/audience, set up like a concert. There can be no argument what is there. My aunt, Gig, was first to speak after the applause.

"That's marvelous."

Almost instantly, as if to lighten the mood, Bob breaks into a kind of updated walking boogie woogie instrumental, joined by

Mark Dorenson playing counterpoint with the mandolin.

"That's great," someone says. "Where'd you pick that up?"

My aunt, who must have still been thinking about "Rising Sun," interjects:

"His insides."

Bob, who is now back in a humorous mode, says:

"The son of the guy who discovered..."

"America," someone else says.

The room fills with laughter.

"All kinds of blues singers. Bessie Smith...," says Bob, and clears his throat.

"Let the frog out," someone jokes.

Bob plays another number, "Highway 51." It's another song on his first album. Again, it seems like a whole rock 'n roll band gathered on the couch. When he finishes you can see he's pleased with himself. If he never sang the song again it wouldn't matter. He has just squeezed out every conceivable drop of whatever it contained.

"You like that?" he says with pride.

"Where'd you pick that up?" another asks from across the room.

"I don't know. Everly Brothers," he replies.

There is a slight lull for a moment as happens at gatherings. Bob deserves a break. For the first time in a while, my mother speaks and his ears pick up.

"Bobby?" she says.

"Oh yes," adds my aunt, Gig.

"Do what?" he asks.

"'This Land." I loved the way you did it at the concert."

"Yes, that was one of the best," Gig affirms.

"You did it magnificently," adds my mother.

Suddenly, Bob realizes Suze is not back yet in her chair and appears flustered, almost panicky. His eyes search the room.

"Where's...?" he says and pauses.

"She'll be right back. She went to the bathroom. She'll be out. She'll be here," says Mom.

Seeing he is anxious about Suze's absence Gig comes up with a quick fix.

"Anne (Marie), sit down while Suze's gone."

Anne-Marie sits down in the wicker chair opposite him. His anxiety has partially abated. He did seem a bit rattled when he looked up and saw Suze wasn't there. His foot starts tapping as he begins flat picking the melody at a medium pace before singing the first verse. Those observing, who would normally join in on the song because it's the most famous American folksong ever, become quiet. No one is joining in on the verses, or the chorus. No one is moving. There is just the steady pounding of Bob's foot on the floor as he goes through each verse and chorus, enunciating each word as if it were an irreplaceable jewel. It was like a new song being heard for the first time; so personal it was hard to imagine he had not written it. Then he sings another verse I had heard him do only once before at his November 4th concert about "Walking a freedom highway." I had never heard anyone else sing that verse. I thought he composed it himself. Only later did I learn that Woody Guthrie had written more than the traditional three verses our fifth-grade elementary school visiting music instructor, Pete Seeger, had taught us. That additional verse was written by Woody, but it fit Bob like a glove. He owned it. Instead of ending the song by singing the last chorus and following it with a quick guitar flourish, he sings the last chorus and then repeats it instrumentally, playing each note individually, letting all the previous verses and choruses sink in.

Later that evening he wrote out the last verse for my mother.

(Additional verse to "This Land Is Your Land")
-From the William Pagel archives-

All is quiet for a moment before the applause and whistles. As the sound dies down the inevitable request is made.

"The harmonica, Bob."

He tries to shrug it off.

"I'm tired, man, I can't."

"I've never heard you play it," says Robbie Workoff, the younger brother of Kevin's girlfriend, Sue.

It's the perfect excuse for Kevin to reenter the conversation with a loud voice saying, "I ain't never heard you play it either and Sonny Terry says you're the best in the country."

Kevin, of course, had heard Bob play the harmonica countless times. It was his way of saying, "Come on and please my girlfriend's brother."

My mother momentarily eases the situation.

"He's thirsty," she says.

"Who's thirsty?" my father asks. "Robert the Dill?"

That was an affectionate name for Bob he sometimes used.

Before anyone can move Robbie is talking about harmonicas again.

"There's some in the case."

"You want some more vermouth?" Mom asks Bob.

"Oh, you want to hear one? Okay. I'll play you one song."

"You have a brace? You have a rig?" asks Robbie.

"Where's Mark (Eastman)?" Bob says.

"Hey, Bobby, how old is Woody's oldest kid?" asks Kevin.

"Fourteen."

Before it gets off track Mark comes over with harmonicas and a harmonica holder.

"Have you got a G?" Bob says.

He puts the harmonica rig around his neck, puts in the harmonica, blows a note to make sure the guitar is in tune with it and goes right into the instrumental. It's an up-tempo folk, bluegrass type melody he's improvising on the spot. While only planning to play about a minute and be done with it he hits on a new harmonica phrase he likes. He wants to polish it to get it just right. He keeps going, repeating it, finally playing it to his satisfaction. It lasts longer than a minute.

Applause. Everyone begins to talk. Kevin's voice cuts through:

"Hey, Bob, can you play 'This Land Is Your Land' again so we can all sing it?"

It is more a statement then a request.

This time, though, Bob is done.

"I can't play that. I can't play that. Why don't you play somethin'?"

That made perfect sense. There were plenty of other guitar players and guitars. They'd all been fed. Let them do some work for a change... And that is exactly what happened. Others picked up guitars. A "This Land Is Your Land" group sing-along was performed. Robbie Workoff got hold of a guitar and, along with Mark Eastman, the whole group did a rendition of "Bells Of Rhymney," "Marching To Trafalgar Square," and some other numbers. The evening's hootenanny was in full swing. I was having a grand old time sitting between Bob and Suze on the couch while they talked to each other and me... like a family.

I don't remember the name on the vermouth bottle, but what happened that night is the only one of its kind and is stored on one, two-sided reel of tape that went spinning around on a little machine that came from across the ocean. If you hear it you may not know exactly what it represents, but you know something is happening...

YES, that celebration was unique in every way. When I reach back into the memories of that evening it warms my heart. I play the recording and hear my parents' voices, a younger me talking with a younger Bob, and Kevin's loud bravado.

Two months earlier the farthest thing from my mouth was a pair of upturned lips.

Professional quality at a popular price!

Mr + Mrs Workoff — Cathy
Gertrude — Allen
Ann Dorsine — David
Eve + Mac — Steve
Peter —
Kevin — Bobby Dylan
Mark Eastman
Ed Bloom
Mark Dorenson
Bobby Workoff
Suzy

Time Chart

TAPE LENGTH	SINGLE TRACK		DUAL TRACK	
	3¾ ips	7½ ips	3¾ ips	7½ ips
600 FT.	30 min.	15 min.	1 hr.	30 min.
900 FT.	45 min.	22½ min.	1 hr. 30 min.	45 min.
1200 FT.	1 hr.	30 min.	2 hr.	1 hr.

SCOTCH
BRAND
Magnetic Tapes

Notice: Buyers shall determine that contents are proper kind for intended use. If defective in the manufacture, labeling, or packaging, contents will be replaced. There are no other warranties, expressed or implied.

Patented under one or more U.S. Patents 2603469, 2711901.

THE TERMS "SCOTCH" AND ITS PLAID DESIGN ARE REGISTERED TRADEMARKS FOR MAGNETIC TAPE MADE IN U.S.A. BY MINNESOTA MINING AND MANUFACTURING COMPANY.

CHAPTER 36:
GOODBYE IS JUST A SEVEN LETTER WORD

The Summer of 1961 was winding down. September was going by day by day. That meant school was going to start soon. One thing that hadn't changed were the comings and goings of all those who had been coming and going. As for my parents... my mother was a bit concerned with what was going to happen when the school year started. How was I going to put my nose to the grindstone and concentrate with everything else going on? My attitude was 'No big deal.' Nothing has to change. I could handle it with no problem. I'm sure, however, everyone has experienced the relationship between parent and child is not always democratic. An amorphous feeling began to envelop me that something was up. I wasn't quite sure what, but when I found out anger is too mild a word for what I felt. I've thought about it off and on from then until now, from every angle, and my opinion hasn't changed. I can still see no justification for the resulting turn of events.

My parents were concerned about my future, my studies, me wanting to go to Harvard. Knowing how stiff the competition was to get accepted there could be no distractions. Things were starting to speed up and get bigger for Bob. His living style, which included all his fellow folksingers' antics was not exactly the conventional atmosphere if you wanted to matriculate inside Ivy walls. Or so my parents thought.

"How can Peter fully concentrate on his studies with Bob still living at 28th St., considering his attachment, loyalty and idolization of him?," I soon learned was their take on things.

My parents were having discussions with Bob without me knowing about it. A determination was reached that I would do better at school if a comfortable way could be found for Bob to relocate to another living situation before the start of the school year. When I was informed he would soon be leaving, and it was explained why, I was dumbfounded. It did not immediately register. When it did my objections came like a tidal wave. Being vocal barely scratches the surface of the maelstrom. I thought it capricious, stupid, ill-timed, misinformed and a complete betrayal. That's the polite version. The most frustrating thing was I knew no matter how I howled, behaved, or what I said, the decision was done. That didn't stop me, though, from making any and every imaginable objection at every turn.

Bob was in awkward position. He had to walk a fine line. Whether or not he agreed with their assessment, it was not his call to make. He may have made some points on my behalf because he knew my position. That was never revealed to me. I couldn't wheedle an objection to my parent's decision out of him. He spent most of his time doing damage control.

"Pete, don't worry about it. It's not that big a deal. I've a couple of places I can stay until I get my own place. Your folks are doing their best for what they think is right for you."

"But what about you?" I would automatically respond.

"Don't worry about me," he would say. "I'll be fine. I know people. Everything is falling into place. Anyway, I'll be back here lots of times. It'll be like I never left because you'll still see me. You know when the school year starts your time is going to be taken up with your friends and your studies. And then there are the girls. You're going to be 16 soon, fighting them off."

He really tried cheer me up. As good as he had always been with his charm, reasoning and support, this was one time it did not completely work on me. It helped dull the pain, but it didn't make it go away. Before the dreaded day was to arrive I had to come to grips with the truth. It WAS going to happen. I just didn't know the exact day. The making of that decision, for me, has always remained the #1 wrong one by my parents...

I will never forget THAT day. It happened one afternoon in mid-September, soon after Bob had come back from his harmonica rehearsal with Carolyn Hester. It was a quiet morning. Mom, Bob and I were around the house. She made both of us breakfast. Bob's sheets on the couch had not yet been straightened out.

"Well, I've got to go," he says.

"Ok. See you later," I answer.

"No, Pete, I mean I've got to go. I found a place."

There they were - the words I hoped never to hear being said.

"It has to be today?" I exclaimed, almost pleading.

"Afraid so. But you know I'll be back soon."

"Yes, Peter. Bobby's made arrangements and they're expecting him in a little while," my mother added.

"Right now?"

"Yes. Everything's been scheduled. I'm going to put away the sheets from his bed after he leaves."

I wanted to say, "Not acceptable. I forbid it," then grab him and tell him he couldn't leave.

Outwardly, I was trying to give as dignified an appearance as I could. Inside, I was crushed, sad, angry and several other emotions. As the seconds clicked by, each click was like a hammer strike nailing a coffin shut, only the body inside was not dead, but paralyzed.

Bob knew what was taking place in my head.

The apartment front door was open with him standing in the outside hallway. He looked at me and my mother.

"You know, Pete's getting pretty good on the guitar, and he really wants a steel string. I know he likes the one I have. The least I can do is give him my guitar as a going away present."

What? I couldn't believe my ears. He was going to give me his 00-17 Martin. My heart went into overdrive. He was serious. It wasn't an empty gesture. He wanted me to have it. What a way to distract my mind from the pain of his exit.

Just as I was about to get all enthusiastic, my mother's voice cut through the air.

"Oh, Bobby, that's so sweet of you to offer, but we couldn't possibly accept it. That's your livelihood. Besides, it's worth money. We know your money is tight. You could get at least $50 for it."

I could not believe my ears... AGAIN. What was my mother doing? He was offering it to me, not her. It was like pouring salt in a wound, then using sandpaper. Here I was trying to hold it together and the boiling point had just been triggered. In about five seconds...

Bob sensed in an instant what was coming. Ever quick witted and caring, he immediately came up with a solution.

"I'm really sorry, Pete, but I'll tell you what. The next guitar I get, when I'm done with it, I promise I'll give you that one. It'll be even better."

"You will, really?"

Then looking him in the eye I said as confidently as I could:

"I'm going to hold you to it."

The intensity of feeling the teenage me experienced in those few moments is easy to remember.

We both watched him as he went down the steps with his guitar case in one hand and his packed suitcase in the other.

When he opened at Gerde's just over a week later he had another guitar. It's the one that appears on the cover of his first album; the one he played at Town Hall and at Newport in July 1963; the same one in Suze's closet in October 1964.

The subject of Bob's departure from our apartment was only brought up once years later. My mother wondered if the right thing was done by having him leave when he did. I made no comment. There was no need. It did, however, resurrect the image of him standing in the open doorway at 28th St., his first sleepover night in mid-May 1961. He was traveling light. He had a guitar case in one hand and a brown, medium sized suitcase in the other; its only contents one piece of underwear. I thought to myself:

"Why the need for the suitcase? Where's the rest of his stuff?"

(Bob's Martin 00-17 – his first acoustic guitar.)

AFTERWORD

Some say I have an amazing memory for details. If you had Bob Dylan in your home when you were 15, treating you like a kid brother, you would remember everything as well. All events did occur as indicated, and all facts presented are accurate. You may not agree with some of the interpretations and conclusions arrived at and that's okay. There is one matter, however, that needs clarification to set the record straight.

The opening quote by Bob that appears at the beginning of the Introduction is from a 1965 interview with Robert Shelton, the man who wrote the September 29, 1961 review for The New York Times. He later wrote a book on Bob called "No Direction Home," first published in 1986. When I finished my first draft it was suggested I look at his book.

I have great respect for Mr. Shelton and his reviews that promoted many upcoming artists over the years and boosted their careers.

Although Bob advised Mr. Shelton to talk with us, for one reason or another, he failed to follow that advise and, as a result, got several facts wrong.

Despite never having personally met my father, or researched his history, Mr. Shelton took it upon himself to describe my father as "a hard drinking, storytelling longshoreman. Where he got that from is anyone's guess...

My father rarely took a drink. He didn't tell stories. His forte was explaining ways of analyzing historical events so they could be put In proper context. That analytic method, his seemingly unlimited knowledge and understanding of history's details completely fascinated and influenced Bob.

Howard "Mac" McKenzie (as previously noted) was one of the founders and first Vice President of the National Maritime Union. He was their chief negotiator. The union represented seamen, the men who worked on the ships, not longshoremen, the men who worked on the docks. Attempts were made on his life by bad actors because he would not comply with certain demands, as well as threats to the personal safety of his family. That's a whole other book.

In 1988 Bruce Springsteen gave the speech when Bob was inducted into the Rock 'n Roll Hall of Fame. No one could have described Bob Dylan's importance and influence, musically and culturally, on his contemporaries and those that came after, better. The way he ended his speech was very poignant and personal. He was, he said, "the older brother I never had."

I was very fortunate. At a very important time Bob was the older brother I did have, albeit temporarily.

On one occasion, in the middle of summer 1961, Bob found my mother sitting next to the floor lamp in the living room reading Robert Graves.

"So, you like Robert Graves, Eve?"

"Yes. He has a gifted use of language," she answered.

"I agree," he replied.

A delving into all things Graves ensued.

FOOTNOTES

1. "Ramblin' Jack Elliott (born 1931), born Elliot Charles Adnopoz, is an American folk singer and a major figure in the early 1960s folk and topical music revival. He was a major influence on many of the young up and coming singers in that era..

2. Cisco Houston (Gilbert Vandone Houston) (1918 – 1961) was a major figure in American folk music noted for his deep, rich bass voice. He worked extensively with Woody Guthrie in the 1940s and fifties.

3. The National Maritime Union was an AFL-CIO sailors' union that functioned from 1937 until 2001 when it merged with the Seafarers International Union.

4. Arlo Davy Guthrie (born 1947) is a folk singer who became popular in the 1960s for "Alice's Restaurant", a modernized talking blues opposing the Viet-Nam War and the draft.

5. Martha Graham (1894-1991) was a major exponent of modern dance. She founded the eponymous Dance Company in 1926 which is still active. Eve McKenzie danced with Martha Graham.

6. Dylan pretended to have grown up in the southwest when he first arrived in New York.

7. Harry Belafonte (born 1921) is an American singer of Jamaican

background who popularized Calypso in the 1950s with songs such as "Jamaica Farewell." He was active in the Civil Rights Movement with Dr. Martin Luther King, jr. and performed at the 1963 Washington march, along with Bob Dylan and others.

8. Sonny Terry (Saunders Teddell or Terrell) (1911-1986) was a well-known black blues harmonica player who usually played with Brownie McGhee. They were popular during the 1950s and sixties folk music revival.

9. Joan Baez (born 1941) is an American folk singer and peace and environmental activist who was Dylan's musical and romantic companion in the middle 1960s.

10. Suze Rotolo (b. 1941) was Dylan's girlfriend from 1961 until 1964 and appears with him on the cover of "Freewheelin." She wrote of her experiences in "A Freewheelin' Time."

11. Congress authorized the Lend-Lease program in 1941 to supersede the Neutrality Laws. It authorized the U.S. to lend or lease war material to allied combatants, especially Great Britain, that they were to return at the end of the war, which was understood to be a fiction. The Soviet Union and other combatants later received Lend-Lease aid.

12. "Tin Fish" was a nickname for torpedoes.

13. Pete Seeger (1919-2014) and the Almanac Singers were left-wing American folk singers. The Almanac Singers, founded by Millard Lampell, included, at various times, Seeger, Lee Hays, Josh White, Sonny Terry, Burl Ives, and others.

14. Paul Robeson (1898-1976) was a major American actor, musical comedy star and political activist. He played football at Rutgers University and became an attorney. He was headed for major stardom when his career ended during the 1950s when he was blacklisted because he was a Communist Party 9member who praised Russia and visited there.

15. Frederick Douglass (1818-1895) began life a slave, escaped and became the major black spokesman and activist before, during and after the Civil War.

16. Leadbelly (Huddie William Ledbetter) (1888-1949) was an American folk singer and activist. He had a hit with the song "Goodnight Irene" shortly before his blacklisting and death.

17. Dave Van Ronk (1936-2002), Mark Spoelstra (1940-2007) and Danny Kalb (born 1942): American folk singers who gained a following during the 1960s folk revival and continued performing afterwards.

18. The New Lost City Ramblers were a 1960s country-folk group featuring Pete Seeger's, half-brother, Mike, John Cohen and Tom Paley. Paley was replaced in 1962 by Tony Schwarz.

19. Harry Bridges (1901-1990) was the Australian-American left-wing head of the International Longshoremen's Association on the west coast. For many years the US government failed in its numerous attempts to deport him because of his politics.

20. John Lee Hooker (1912 - 2001) was a black blues-jazz singer-guitarist who became popular during the folk revival and

performed until the end of his life.

21. The McCarthy Witch Hunts refers to the period from 1947 until 1960 known as the McCarthy Era, when anti-communist hysteria, much of it ill-founded, gripped the U.S. Joseph McCarthy (1921-1957) was a U.S. Senator from Wisconsin from 1947 until his death in 1957, when he was censured by the Senate. It particularly affected movies and television and contributed to President Lyndon Johnson's decision in 1965 to transform the Viet-Nam War into a major conflict.

ABOUT THE AUTHOR

Peter McKenzie is an artist, musician, and writer based in New York City. He attended the city's High School of Music and Art and graduated with honors from Harvard College in 1967. After studying architecture at the Harvard Graduate School of Design, he traveled to Europe, spending time in Paris and Amsterdam, where he played in a rock-and-roll band. Back home, Peter established a successful career as a graphic artist, book designer and illustrator. He never gave up his love of playing music, at one point running a recording studio. He can often be found with a guitar, harmonica or other instrument in hand. In addition to being an expert in high-end vintage watches, he has served as a consultant to collectors and auction houses, including Sotheby's, verifying the authenticity and provenance of Bob Dylan manuscripts.

ACKNOWLEDGEMENTS

In alphabetical order are those whose assistance and encouragement helped make this book possible. I thank them one and all. If I've unintentionally left someone out that will be corrected at the earliest opportunity.

For their editing skills:
  Katherine Brennan
  Harris Friedberg
  Robert Furman
  Jesse Kornbluth
  Susan Workoff Lesser

Special thanks to:
  Mitch Blank
  Bob Dylan
  Bill Pagel
  Dominick Romano

Additional thanks to:
  Blythe Carey
  Howard Harrison
  Joseph Klein
  Rosemarie Picone
  Robert Post

Made in the USA
Columbia, SC
01 November 2024

45477795R00152